W. R. Kiefer

Stony Point Illustrated

An account of the early settlements on the Hudson, with traditions and relics of the

revolution, and some genealogical records of the present inhabitants

W. R. Kiefer

Stony Point Illustrated
An account of the early settlements on the Hudson, with traditions and relics of the revolution, and some genealogical records of the present inhabitants

ISBN/EAN: 9783337237721

Printed in Europe, USA, Canada, Australia, Japan

Cover: Foto ©Andreas Hilbeck / pixelio.de

More available books at **www.hansebooks.com**

STONY POINT ILLUSTRATED.

AN ACCOUNT OF THE

EARLY SETTLEMENTS ON THE HUDSON

—WITH—

Traditions and Relics of the Revolution,

AND SOME

GENEOLOGICAL RECORDS OF THE PRESENT INHABITANTS.

Dedicated to the Descendants of the Revolutionary Fathers.

Edited and Published by Rev. W. R. Kiefer.

NEW YORK:
Z. R. BENNETT, PRINTER, 76 CORTLANDT STREET.
1888.

COPYRIGHT
1888,
BY W. R. KIEFER.

INTRODUCTION.

BY J. J. SMITH D. D.

It is not the object of the writer of this book to confine the attention of the reader to any one line of thought so as to make a specialty of any particular class of facts, as would a writer on commercial affairs make the national exchange of commodities and the laws of trade his theme; or as would an ecclesiastical historian dwell exclusively upon matters connected with the church; or as the military historian would confine himself to wars, campaigns, strategetical movements of armies, and battles upon land and sea; but in the selection of events the author has evidently sought to group and combine the leading local facts of this town, both historical and biographical, together with narratives, incidents, traditions and illustrations that cannot fail to be deeply interesting, especially to the people of Stony Point and its vicinity, covering, as it does, more or less of the whole period of our national existence.

Besides, this work can hardly fail to interest the children also, inasmuch as it speaks of persons, many of whom they have already become more or less interested in as neighbors and friends, while some sustain the more endearing relationship of kindred. In addition to this it treats of events that have occurred principally within a district with which they are themselves familiar, and which has already become endeared to them by their every day associations.

INTRODUCTION.

This consideration is of special importance to parents, because the human mind is so constituted that it must be, of necessity, occupied in the pursuit of some object, and consequently if it is not directed by a guiding hand into proper channels, it will seek such amusements as may lead directly to indulgence and dissipation. Such a book as this, considered simply in the light of amusement, possesses a very great advantage over the numerous publications of mere fiction, that in too many instances inflame the imagination and excite the worst passions. In this way the morals of thousands of the rising generation are permanently corrupted, if not destroyed. It is because of this fact that parents should see to it that such books are put into their hands as will instruct as well as amuse, and which are morally pure. Such a book we have in the "STONY POINT ILLUSTRATED."

PREFACE.

It is the purpose of the author of the following pages to preserve for the generations to come Revolutionary and home pictures of Stony Point; also, some of the characteristics of the people. If the descendants of the present families who shall live here an hundred years from this time shall read this book with as much interest as its author takes in the writing and publication, our labor will have been amply rewarded.

Having spent four years on these Revolutionary grounds, which are sacred to every true American, and are being more and more visited by historians and military students for their classic and historic interest, we feel that we should do violence to the promptings of our patriotic impulses not to note at least a few of the important features which have daily come to our notice.

The map which forms the frontispiece to this volume is in part a reprint from the original British surveys, and which had been printed for Wm. Faden, Geoghrapher to the King, March 1st, 1781. A perfected survey was procured from field notes made by Prof. L. Wilson of Haverstraw. The improvements on the map were by the author after a special study of the entire field.

How peculiarly fitting that the signal officer of the day of the semi-centennial celebration of "The Storming" should be a man of the same name as the man who commanded the advance regiment that entered the main redoubt in company with Brigadier General Wayne! His name was Febriger, and when the colors were to be waved as a signal for the ships' guns to fire this same Febriger, a young and gallant Lieutenant, performed that most honorable duty.

General Ward, we are told, was here as chief director of the attempt to explain "The Storming." The day was so extremely hot that any attempt at an action which would require great exertion would have been hazardous. The writer was present and overheard the officers in a dispute as to who should command, and as to how to proceed. Their ideas of the real assault were the most confused.

There are persons still living here who shook hands with veterans of the capture of Stony Point. In a very few years these living witnesses will be silenced forever, and the important links of testimony which they can furnish will be missing, never to be recalled.

We cherish with exalted respect and grateful memory the recital of these *traditional* deeds of the departed heroes of the brilliant achievement, and to record them in this volume is our proudest work—purely, too, a labor of love.

We gratefully acknowledge the assistance of C. B. Story and E. A. Thompson in the preparation of the work which is now submitted to the reader.

THE AUTHOR.

CONTENTS.

PART I.

	PAGE
CHAPTER I—Monumental History.	9
" II—Our Historic Ground.	11
" III—The Primitive Inhabitants.	13
" IV—The First White Settlers.	21
" V—The Capture of Stony Point.	30
" VI—The Forgotten Monuments of our Heroes.	42
" VII—The Treason of Arnold.	46
" VIII—Operations on the Hudson.	54
" IX—Traditions of the Revolution.	60
" X—Relics.	77
" XI—The Celebration.	85

PART II.

CHAPTER I—The Prospects of the Place.	101
" II—Fishing.	104
" III—The Geology of Stony Point.	106
" IV—Music.	111
" V—The Churches.	113
" VI—Registration.	123
" VII—Biographical Sketches.	129
" VIII—Self-Made Men.	149

Stony Point Illustrated.
Part I.

STONY POINT ILLUSTRATED.

CHAPTER I.

MONUMENTAL HISTORY—ITS GREAT UTILITY.

BEFORE the introduction of writing, past events were recorded with the chisel on the rock. The ancient Egyptians and Mexicans represented ideas by the use of pictures or engravings of celestial bodies, the human body, animals, &c. They were most commonly cut in relief on the face of rock, but sometimes they were traced out with a reed with coloring of vegetable and mineral inks, known in the Glyptic art as polychrome. Those representing simple ideas are called *ideaographs*, and those expressing sounds are called *phonetics*.

In the days when men lived five hundred years, and nearly twice that length of time, writing and monumental engraving were not so essential to the preservation of events. The art of writing was more fully developed when mans' days were cut down to " three score and ten."

Monuments are the most convincing historians of all the mediums which men employ for the transmission of events.

On the face of the rock in Kosciusko's Garden at West Point are engraved on the granite immortal words which are read by every visitor. All the epitaphs of the park are of peculiar interest, while in the cliff of the rock near by is still legible the mark of a cannon ball, which, it is said, was fired from an English gun on the river, while the General lay sleeping on a narrow ledge only a few inches below the spot where the missile took effect.

On the Palisade of the Rocky Falls, on the beautiful Delaware River, about fifty miles north of Philadelphia, may still be seen an indenture with a piece of iron wedged in it, as the result of a floating wreck of some boat which was swept by on the wild and maddened stream during the great freshet of 1861; that mark on the face of the rock will for all time, that the granite remains, indicate the height to which the river had risen. Monuments are still standing which prove the high-water mark of a freshet in the same river in 1841.

These spots, chiseled in the natural rock, either by hand or by nature, mark certain events which the student of history reads with profoundest interest; they form the very alphabet and language of his investigation of causes and events; to him they present true historic beauty and are living imprints of artificial and natural causes.

Many are the noble deeds which the faithful forefathers of our people wrought for their posterity. All about us are fruits which their hands have cultivated. Of few, if any, can a memoir be found. Why should not we record for generations to come, the affairs that occupy *our* attention, the customs that enslave or enrich our citizens, the haps and mishaps that are incidental to *our* community—that excite *us* to sadness or pleasure—and thus preserve from decay what would otherwise remain unknown to those who shall follow us and know only that we once lived.

CHAPTER II.

OUR HISTORIC GROUND.

NO PLACE on the noble River of Hudson can more justly boast of important historic data, or more enchanting scenery, than our Revolutionary Stony Point; and yet we fear that in all the records of our national civilization, or the annals of the struggle of our nation for independence, no place of similar historic value is more meagerly treated. A heritage so grandly sanctified by the bravery and true devotion of our patriot fathers should elicit the tenderest interest of the immediate descendants, if not, as well, of the most remote citizen of the land.

A feeling of sadness steals over the writer as he approaches the duty of gathering the treasures of history which the departed fathers, and mothers, too, have earned for us. How much to be lamented that some kind survivor did not earlier write up their heroic deeds! How deep and sad was the neglect of so tender a work!

How many a broken home would be cheered in their pilgrimage if they could turn to some biographical cabinet and read the life of their departed! Alas! they can with the poet exclaim:

> "The departed! the departed!
> They visit us in dreams,
> And they glide above our memories
> Like shadows over streams;
> But where the cheerful lights of home
> In constant luster burn,
> The departed, the departed
> Can never more return!"

How many a devoted mother, having failed to procure a photograph of her darling child, mourns the more bitterly over the unpardonable neglect in the event of the child's death! Had she the opportunity to improve again, nothing would hinder her from the possession. Many valuable treasures of thought are buried in the grave. With a few remembered sayings the obituary of many is completed; whereas at the cost of a few hours of pleasant labor a volume of useful and comforting memoir could have been preserved.

It was to meet this want, in part, that these pages were prompted to be penned. The limit of our design and space forbidding anything more than a bare synopsis of such obituary of deceased persons as may incidentally be met with, our object shall be chiefly to record the prominent and worthy deeds of persons who live among us now.

Of the character of the ancestors of these people we shall speak more full in succeeding chapters, especially of those of whom the poet said:

"Fair Science frowned not on his humble birth."
(Nor would we)
"Further seek his merits to disclose,
"Nor draw his frailties from their dread abode,
"Where they alike in trembling hope repose—
"The bosom of his Father and his God."

The shortness of the time since our village was founded or began its material development would allow us to embrace more persons in the memorial department of the geneological record; and yet for want of space, and because many otherwise well-disposed persons failed to return the blanks sent them, our record must be brief in the case of many.

CHAPTER III.

THE PRIMITIVE INHABITANTS—THE INDIANS.

WE WILL notice the natives of the primitive forests as having prior claims. The Indians were ahead of us all. Before the colonists disputed, with sword and musket, the invasion of the enemy of our national freedom, the red man sat surrounding the fires of his rude wigwam on these sacred shores. Many generations of these nomadic people are probably entombed in our sandy hillocks.

Long before our ancestors, devoted to immediate and future settlement on our beautiful bay, sauntering Indians from the banks of the Mohawk made their extended journeys to our sloping shores and drew their canoes on our silent beach. Here Powontonamo, the eagle of his tribe, with his laden canoe, broke the smooth surface of the "Tappan Zee," and held communion with the chief of the Algonquin tribe. During thousands of moons the delighted and simple natives danced beneath broad oaks which spread for canopy along these shores of the "River of the Mountain;" here tribe after tribe sung their warlike deeds to their children and harvested the fruits of nature's orchards and vineyards of neighboring hills. Even here on these grounds where *our* temples stand and God is worshipped, the wild-man also bowed to the "Great Spirit."

"The same stars that sank and reposed behind the primitive shelter of the dusky inhabitant, shine over us now. Beneath the same sun that shines on us the Indian hunter pursued the panting deer; gazing on the same moon that smiles on you, the Indian lover wooed his dusky mate. Here the wigwams' blaze beamed on the tender and helpless, and the council fire glared on the wise and daring. Now they dipped their noble limbs in your sedgy lake (bay) and now they paddled the light canoe along your rocky shores. Here they warred; the echoing whoop, the bloody grapple, the defying death song—all were here: and when the tiger strife was over, here curled the smoke of peace."

Two hundred and fifty winters ago sledges laden with the skins of the otter and beaver glided over the ice of our Hudson, while but a few years later troops of New Amsterdam (now New York City,) ascended the river to protect Esopus from the attack of the Indians. The Iroquois Indians were early associated with the English government of New York State. As early as 1685, Governor Dongan opposed the enslaving of the Iroquois Indians to a religion which would have allied them to the French nation, with whom this same tribe afterward became seriously involved in war. In 1684 the governors of New York and Virginia held a war council with the "Five Nations" at Albany, and secured a treaty of peace. Up to that time the most of the country around here was an unbroken forest and was part of the domain of the swarthy dwellers of the wood. Sachem after Sachem for centuries fished in our streams, shot his arrows across our ravine, and snared the grouse of the native glens.

These shores, the most accessible from the sea and highland stream, and the most natural outlet to the great wooded district on the west, witnessed many an extraordinary Indian scene. This broad, wealthy, healthful plateau had for them, as for us, elysian charms. Here cupid's lustful eye looked long and insatiate; here, stranger than all, the halting trail encamped on soil which glacial ages had deposited only for the white man, while the unconscious "lords of the domain" were satisfied with their stone implements and humble ornaments gathered from the banks of the Shatemuc River as our Hudson was called.

The Champac tree of India is probably not more sacred to the Buddhist worshipper than our venerable cedars were to the canoe builders, the Minsies of the bay shore. Many specimens of those durable barks were long years after objects of common interest to the early white settlers. The Dutch called them Sanhecan barks.

Here on rocks and terraces they knotted the meshes of the fishing seine or counted wampum to mark the departing seasons or note the great events of their savage lives. Here the story of a man saved by a canoe foreshadowed the orthodox history of a general flood.

In the grand forest which then shaded and beautified the beach from Grassy Point to Haverstraw, Indian boys and girls played at games so peculiar to their forest life. The bald vacancy of the present locality is in pitiful contrast to the green fringe of trees that then ornamented the noble river.

But, alas! these hunting lands and play grounds of the red race are here despoiled for savage and enlightened alike forever. The rocks of our minor Palisades and the towering "Thor" no longer send back the echoing of the laugh of the savage juveniles or the songs of the chase or gathering corn by the sons and daughters of the "Haverstroos" of these woods. Not even a tree or mound is left to mark the spot where the red man rested from the trail on the beautiful banks of the Dutch Mauritus. The winding Minescongo still flowing in her primitive silence from eddy to eddy, from meadow to mead, meandering in the shadow of the June grasses, slowly moves to mingle at last with the waters of the great Hudson at the extreme north of the peninsular of Grassy Point; but the aboriginies, the old, the young, the playful, the grave, with their arts of the field and pastimes of the camp, are gone. Two centuries have changed the character of a great continent, and blotted forever from its face nearly a whole peculiar people. They live only in the stories that charm our children. Their melancholy sigh is heard dying across the plains of the far west.

"They waste us; ay, like April snow,
  In the warm noon we shrink away;
And fast they follow as we go
  Toward the setting day,—
Till they shall fill the land, and we
  Are driven into the western sea."

Bryant.

Conquered, yet untamed, the American Indians were early provided with moral instruction. Who knows but chiefs walked these banks who saw Elliot's Indian Bible. Nearly a century and a half ago, David Brainerd preached to tribes in the State of New Jersey who occasionally gathered from the upper Hudson. The dialects of the Esquiman and Algonquin stretched eastward from the Rocky Mountains, covering the vast region from Behring's Strait to Greenland, and southward to the St. Lawrence, and was according to good authority the main language along the Atlantic coast, while the earliest students of philology trace kindred methods of exchange of thought among all the various Indian families. How wisely has it been said: "And all this has passed away. Across the ocean came a Pilgrim bark, bearing the seeds of life and death; the former were sown for you; the latter sprang up in the path of the simple native."

A few illustrations of the Indian language will be interesting to our youthful readers. The Sioux Indian draws the right hand across the throat; by this he signifies "cut-throats" or murderers. One tribe touches the left breast, the region of the heart, and is understood even by another tribe to mean good-hearted. To describe a chief, the mute native raises his finger above his head, and with it makes a reverse motion, raising or lowering the finger according to the size of the person he is describing. An amusing sign to express a woman is for the speaker to draw the fingers slowly through the hair, something after the fashion of the hair exhibitors on Fourteenth street, New York, and then, by adding the wave sign, a movement of the hand from front to the right, as one of us would do in depreciation of a thing, the person addressed understands the speaker to mean that the person he is describing is not a woman, but a man. He would be understood to be describing a female by the combing process, and a male by the sign of combing long hair and the depreciating sign of *no* or *not* added. Rivers are indicated by the moving along of the extended hand, which conveys the idea of a running stream. If no water abounds the savage makes the sign of water, and follows it by the sign of no. If he wishes to own the garment or implement of another, he rubs the forefinger over the nose. If he wishes to show that he had a good crop of corn or fruit he gives the sign of the article, whether grain or fruit, and then proceeds to a motion of heaping up with the hands. The hollow hand brought to the lips, conveys the idea of thirst. Cleanliness is shown by rubbing the palm of the right hand over that of the left, in an outward direction toward the fingers. This sign language is common to all the tribes of the American Indians, and was pretty well read by the first settlers here.

England early provided for schooling the native Indians. A school called "Wheelock School," in New Hampshire, was originally instituted for the benefit of the Indians; finally, Dartmouth College, from whose classic and scientific halls such men as Daniel Webster and Rufus Choate graduated, grew out of it.

Grammar was taught the Rhode Island Indians as early as 1650. Thus the foundations of educational institutions were contemporary with the introduction of civilization among the New England aboriginal tribes. They will rise in the judgment and bless the name of Roger Williams, who taught them the first rudimentary elements of the laws of their language, and through them the knowledge of the true God.

Canadian Indians are still singing religious songs compiled in their language in the early days of mission work among the Mohawk natives, by the missionaries of the Methodist Episcopal Church. John Wesley labored among them in the south, in 1736.

Wm. Bradford, publisher of the *New York Gazette*, about 1715, printed the book of "Common Prayer" in the Indian language.

The following soliloquy on the finding of an arrow-head, was compiled by the Rev. J. J. Smith, D. D. It is by his kind permission we insert two stanzas of the poem.

> "Thou relic of the long gone past,
>   Memento of a race
> Now either gone or fading fast,
>   Whose history none may trace,
> Thou tellest of a former day,
>   When on hills, plains and all,
> The shadows of vast forests lay,
>   Like a dark, dreary pall."

Who can say but that one hundred and sixty years ago, these shores reverberated with the voice of prayer, which arose from the lips of the swarthy sons of those forest wilds, in utterance of the same petitions that to-day arise from our altars, and the lips of the red man said: "Our Father who art in heaven." But, alas, those infantile mutterings are stilled like the ripples of their plying canoe. Shadows of long oblivion hang over that early forest geneology. The war-whoop of the maurauding Iroquois, the Indian of Indians, who called themselves "People of the long house," have slept for ages in the narrow house of their forest graves. The Mohawks, the Algonquins, the Tappans, the Minsies, the Haverstroos and all the sub-tribes and families of the red men, have melted away forever. The foot that once lightly pressed our native heather and brushed the morning dew along Flora Falls, has long mingled with the dust to which we are all tending.

Here on the sides of the canyons are still to be found the offspring of the ancient pines of which Garland wrote in the beautiful stanza which follows, among which we may imagine we hear the voice of the departed American Indian:

> "O, sunless deeps of northern pines,
>   O, broad snow laden arms of fir,
> Dim aisles, where wolves slip to and fro,
>   And noiseless wild deer swiftly skirr.
> O, home of wind songs, wild and grand,
>   As suits thy mighty strains, O harp,
> On which the north wind lays his hand,
>   I walk thy pungent glooms once more,
> And shout amid thy stormful roar."

WEST SHORE RAILROAD DEPOT.

CHAPTER IV.

FIRST WHITE SETTLERS.

ANTEDATING the Revolution we note some of the early characteristics of the first settlers from foreign shores; especially would we trace the origin of the religious and moral proclivities of the people.

Their morals have a noble ancestral history of Puritan stock. The early settlers were deeply read in the divine book; as inflexible as their wills were their convictions of righteousness. Their nativities were Dutch, French and a few Swedes; hence the sturdiness of many of the oldest inhabitants when encountered by principles not founded in righteousness. Later, the people were leavened by English thought and habit, though the predominant bent of public thought was Hollandish.

Out of their sentiments of supreme love of and loyalty to the great political principles of their day, they laid well the foundations of civil and moral excellence now seen so broad and deep in the present conglomerate people.

Dutch were one of the trio of nations that settled on our "North River," and traded with the savages in "skins of the deer, the otter and the beaver." Meantime settlements were spreading with their leavening civilizations from the Atlantic sea-board to westward, southward and to the North Sea. The grants of foreign powers took each their own trend; the English westward toward the golden shores; the French from St. Lawrence to the Great Gulf, and the Spaniards to the dark, cold Arctic Ocean. "In the centre of the wild, trackless, shaggy continent lay our Empire

State. The vast unexplored forests were wrapped in savage slumber."

The following is a picture of our crude native land as drawn by Parkman:

"On the banks of the James was a nest of woebegone Englishmen, a handful of fur-traders at the mouth of the Hudson, and a few shivering Frenchmen among the snow-drifts of Acadia; while amid the still wilder desolation, Champlain upheld the banner of France over the icy rock of Quebec. These were the advance guard of civilization—the messengers of promise to a desert continent."

New York was the architrave of the national building. It was more: it formed the base of the superstructure. While the composition of its moral granite was made of the solid, plodding Holland character, the manufacturing genius of England, and the romantic sprightliness of French etiquette, its cementing religious virtues were extractions of French Hugunot, the quint essence of English formality, and the sturdiness of Dutch perseverance.

Our present Stony Point society rests on pillars of the above construction, while ancestral names bear the image of the foregoing progenitors.

Ireland, so prolific of noble genius and native wit and eloquence, has likewise given of her purest and most honored sons to the development of our local resources, and the spread of our industrial energies.

As father Marquette, who died on the banks of the Arkansas in search of the "Father of Waters," in 1673, was buried near the mouth of the river which bears his name, and as Champlain, captivated by the charms of Canada, longed to plant there an empire of his people, but died on the St. Lawrence and was buried on the soil he had won, so many of the sons of "Erin" now sleep in the midst of their toils hard by "Mt. Repose," and rest in the soil which wooed them from their fatherland—the salubrious isle of their nativity—to seek the wealth and freedom of these lucrative shores. They found here the veritable "Curragh Kildare" of the Hudson, with her broad, deep clay beds—the emerald "Bog Allen" of the Upper Netherlands.

RILEY & CLARK'S BRICK-YARD.

While many sons and daughters of that British Isle rest here from their toil, honorable and long is the list of the living who still press the pursuits of their illustrious departed. Of those living among us it is just to say their sturdy muscle largely holds the financial grip of the immense brick industry of our town. It would be simple injustice to their economical and faithful toil to omit a record of them in this volume. Lads, who "patted and edged" brick in these yards a score of years ago, are now among the most successful manufacturers, and dwell amidst affluence and high social surroundings, with the means to live in imperial style. Their civility, as neighbors, and their manly dealing in business, have won for them well merited esteem. Inclining mainly to the Catholic faith religiously, they have had liberal success. Their friendly relations to all other evangelical churches have gained for them a sympathy which extends to their material aid in all their ecclesiastical work for which they are noted in a pre-eminent degree. No undertaking of the writer has ever received any kind of disregard by those kind hearted people. Our subscription lists are well sprinkled with Celtic names, while the bricks in many charitable institutions and Christian churches are stamped with initials of Irish manufacturers.

So these men have "pitched their tents before the city," and as a distinguished memorial of their prosperity have erected their churches, saying: "Eliocani—toward him are mine eyes."

Devotion to God was so closely connected with devotion to their country, among the struggling colonists, that it is easy to see how the zeal for the one was inflamed by the other.

At the news of the great victory over Cornwallis at the fall of Yorktown, Virginia, an event which in effect recovered the whole country to the poor starving men, women and children of this undeveloped country, high transports of exhultation burst upon the colonists, and the great victory was celebrated in every part of the union. Under a devout sense of signal Divine help in this extraordinary time, Washington requested his army to observe a special day of religious service, and an order read to the troops said that "all the troops should engage in it with serious deportment, and that sensibility of heart which the surprising and particular interposition of Providence in their favor claimed."

By an act of Congress then assembled in the city of Philadelphia, the 13th day of December was set apart as a day of prayer; and as an example to our fathers and mothers, that dignified body of warriors and public men went in procession to a church in that city "to return thanks to Almighty God for the signal success of the American arms."

Succeeding Andross, whom the people looked upon as a tyrant, Colonel Thomas Dongan, a Roman Catholic, was appointed Governor of the Empire State. It was during his administration, by the advice of the Quaker, Wm. Penn, that the first assembly was called and the first " Charter of Liberties " was formulated.

The freedom of thought and legislative privilege enjoyed by the fathers must ever be accorded in large measure to the liberal minded Dongan, without whose consent, at least, the following immortal legislation would not have been made:

" Supreme legislative power shall *forever reside* in the Governor, Council and people in General Assembly; that every freeholder and freeman may vote for Representatives without restraint; that no freeman shall suffer but by judgment of his peers, and all trials shall be by a jury of twelve men; that no tax shall be assessed on any pretence whatever, but by the consent of the Assembly; that no seaman or soldier shall be quartered on the inhabitants against their will; that no martial law shall exist; and that no person *professing faith in God by Jesus Christ*, shall at any time be in any way disquieted or questioned for any difference of opinion in matters of religion."

Again, in 1698, the Governorship of New York fell on Bellamont, an Irish peer, whose strong will and unimpeachable integrity did much for our people, and unlike the intolerant Fletcher, who labored with great zeal in endeavoring to establish the English church, allowed that freedom to worship God, for which the Pilgrim Fathers had sought these shores.

The religious sentiment which still adheres to our community had culminated during the Colonial existence of our ancestors in fixed Puritanical principles and customs. As the government of the people had more and more become English, that portion of society that were of Dutch and Swedish origin did not readily take to the ceremonies of the ritualistic English church. In fact, the

Whig and Tory spirit that agitated the people politically during the Revolution, entered largely into the ecclesiastical and religious life of the early families. If an English settler entertained Tory sentiments, he endorsed high-church aristocracy—English establishment notions. If he was of the Puritanical sect, he turned his English enthusiasm and political views to the best account toward the success of the Church of the Reformation. This was mainly true of all the respective nationalities, who represented the mixed settlement of the town.

The same ambition that obtained in Scotland, in 1625, when King James attempted to establish a conformity in worship and discipline between the churches of the two kingdoms, (Scotland and England,) was shown by the Royal authorities in the days of the colonists here. The same zeal which actuated the Scottish nobility and the common people of Scotland to maintain separate church and "kirk," also obtained among the Puritan people of this country.

While the Dutch, who settled in New Amsterdam and extended their trading-posts to our cove, along the river, were mainly direct descendants from Holland proper, others of them were from French Huguenot descent. These latter were chiefly found among the more religious families, and from whom can be traced the lineage of some of our best citizens.

Hume, the English historian, said the name "Puritan" stood for three parties. "There were the political Puritans, who maintained the highest principles of civil liberty; the Puritans in discipline, who were averse to the ceremonies and Episcopal government of the Church; and the doctrinal Puritans, who rigidly defended the speculative systems of the first reformers."

In the spirit of the above exposition of a Puritan, the philosophic reader will discover the true germs of Republicanism, which

W. TOMPKINS—REVOLUTIONARY HOUSE.

afterward culminated in the platform of the Revolutionary Whig party, from which the Republican party sprang, as to its incipient principles. Few persons, even among the educated, can show the real difference between Democracy as it was originally, and Republicanism as it really is, when properly defined. As independence and freedom are terms of similar meaning, so Democracy and Republicanism, when properly explained, convey but one meaning—that not to be ruled by royalty, but by themselves; but as people cannot rule themselves without organization and governmental authority vested in some one of their number, either party must adopt some form of government based on representative choice. Both are representative systems as against an arbitrary system of royal ruling.

As the political parties grew, naturally they would take on differing views of national questions. The greed of power, the love of money, desire for luxuries, suggested political bribery. The desire to get a livelihood out of other persons' labors, took shape in certain great sectional economies. Cotton became king. Money became synonymous with power. Human labor became capital. Men and women were bought for their labor value, and were propagated and imported for that purpose. Ownership of souls gave power of their disposal and treatment. Education assured the rising generations of a livelihood, whether honorable or otherwise. Emigration soon created national jealousy. Some factions opposed the coming of so many foreigners, and so the national questions increased in number and importance. Politics became God, and God interfered, and contending armies of the opposing factions engaged in the deadly strife. Civil war covered the land.

However, so strongly had the minds of the colonists become imbued with the spirit of independence, both from what they had seen in the imperial ruling of the foreign king at home, and what they saw of his rule by the Governors of his appointment in the colonies, that, wherever they settled in the new country, they inculcated on those under them, their own opinions and spirit of self-government.

As proof of this, we have but to read the following extract from the writings of Graham, who said: "It was for no ordinary people that the land (America) was reserved, and of no common qualities or vulgar superiority that it was ordained to be the prize." The language of the emigrating people themselves, in their request to King James for his approval of the embarkation, was proof of this growing desire for civil and religious liberty. In unmistakable words they said: "We are well weaned from the delicate milk of the mother country, and inured to the difficulties of a strange land. We are knit together in a strict and sacred bond, by virtue of which we hold ourselves bound to take care of the good of each

TOMPKINS COVE METHODIST CHURCH.

other, and of the whole. It is not with us as with other men, whom small things discourage, or cause to wish themselves at home again."

How full of meaning is the following old Pilgrim song, when applied to settlers of our town:

"Ay, call it holy ground,
　The soil where first they trod.
　They have left unstained what (here) they found;
　　Freedom to worship God."

From Harper's Magazine. Copyright, 1879, by Harper & Brothers.

GENERAL ANTHONY WAYNE.

CHAPTER V.

THE STORMING OR CAPTURE OF STONY POINT FORT.

AS WE look from the window of our study, which commands a magnificent view of the entire promontory from west to east, on the cherished ruins of the old fort, and on the same placid waters at its base, where war ships once had anchored, and then read the letter, which Wayne, in broken English, penned as his first report to General Washington, a few minutes after the carnage had ceased, and while dying captives and vanquished foes were begging dismantled at his feet, we copy for the readers of centuries to come, the following immortal words:

"STONY POINT, 2 o'clock A. M., 16 July, 1779.
DEAR GENERAL:

The fort and garrison, with Colonel Johnson, are ours. Our officers and men behaved like men who are determined to be free.

Yours most sincerely,

ANTHONY WAYNE."

The reader is now sufficiently interested to want a fuller account of the great event. It was at midnight. The hour was a sad token of the troubled condition of the country at that time. It was a time of terrible despondency. Much of the wealth and aristocracy of the colonies was almost prepared to compromise with the British. Congress was doubtful. Washington had been in command of the patriots with varying success, since his appointment, May 10, 1775. He had had some decided victories, but more failures. Washington's faith never wavered, but sustained him, because he knew his cause was just. He had solidified his purposes by prayers and tears. During his stay at Valley Forge he was overheard, on bended knee, in a ravine, pleading with God for victory. Mr. Potts, who happened to overhear the prayer, related the solemn incident to his wife, and remarked: If there was any one to whom the Lord would listen, it was George Washington, and that under such a commander their independence was certain. Pennsylvania and Massachusetts had, through distinguished delegations, sought to predjudice Congress against Washington. England, tired and frightened, sought by overtures and costly bribes to ask reconciliation.

Benjamin Franklin was at that time embassador to France, and secured assistance from that nation, but large numbers of the colonists had joined the Tories with the hope that in the event of the victory of England, they would be spared. It was a question now of life and death. A company of natives, some of them citizens of our town, had united in the defence of the fort, after its evacuation by Washington, the last of May, less than two months before its recapture, of which we are writing.

As an index of the public feeling that Washington would fail, we quote from Wayne's letter to his brother-in-law, Sharpe Delaney, Philadelphia, penned at Spring Steels an hour before the assault, midnight, July 15, 1779, in which Wayne says as follows: "You have often heard me default the supineness and unworthy torpidity into which Congress were lulled, and that it was my decided opinion this would be a sanguinary campaign in which many of the choicest spirits and much of the best blood in America would be lost, owing to the parsimony and neglect of Congress. If ever any prediction was true, it is this; and if ever a great and good man was surrounded with a choice of difficulties, it is General Washington. I fear the consequences. I see clearly that he will be impelled to make *other* attempts and efforts in order to save his country; that his numbers will not be adequate, and that he may fall a sacrifice to the folly and parsimony of our *worthy rulers.*"

It is plain to see that a great and desperate hour had come. To meet the present emergency a gigantic stroke of military prowess must be made. Washington saw that a crisis had arrived. Great and farseeing strategy was revolving behind the broad brow of the Herculean General. He looked about for generalship of the sturdiest type, on account of the heavy blow about to be struck, so that the British arm, which held in its grip of steel the redoubts of Verplanck's and Stony Point, with their out works, might be broken. At high and commanding points above the garrisons and out of reach of the unsuspecting Tories and foreign troops on the river fortifications, Gen. Washington had improvised temporary forts. Meanwhile the marshaling of selected troops had placed under the command of the gallant Wayne a certain number of the most reliable men of the army. A reconnoitering system had been carried on for at least a month before the attack. The works, the contour of the land, the natural and artificial defences, the tide water obstructions of the point, together with the advantageous prospects for fleet attack from the north and south sides of the promontory, had received the careful personal investigation of the Commander in Chief, as well as of the head Engineers and the shrewdest Generals, even to the picked men who were to lead the van of the volunteers on the fatal night. Every precaution of a well planned campaign had been taken, and General Wayne allowed his own set time when a "favorable opportunity for striking an advantageous stroke" should be presented.

Washington had, on the 6th of July, made a personal examination of the enemy's garrison, and pronounced the "works formidable," but entertained the hope that on a further examination they might be "found accessible." His knowledge, however, in the nature of things, must be limited as to the enemy's fortification of the hill; for as Wayne had offered to attend the General on the 2nd of July, in a personal inspection of the works, under a strong guard of the "Light Corps," it is pretty clearly evident

From Harper's Magazine.   Copyright, 1879, by Harper & Brothers

THE BATTLE OF STONY POINT.

that the examination was, to say the least of it, made under considerable danger. Anyone acquainted with the geography of the elevation will see with what extreme difficulty an inspection by day-light must be attended. The extreme length of the land from the causeway and rivulet, which bound it on the west, to the bold, high, rocky face, which juts into the river toward Verplanck's Point on the opposite side, is probably a full half mile. On the ridge and undulating ground are a number of rough, rocky hills, which would form clever fortifications with the least engineering, while natural openings occurred between them. On careful study, some of these hills reveal traces of rifle pits and breast-works.

Entirely contrary to the common opinion, the front of the enemy's fortification was to the west, and that the southern exposure of the garrison was the right flank; and, as Washington states in his note of the 9th, to Wayne, a British deserter gave information of a "sandy beach on the south side, running along the flank of the works, and only obstructed, 'at that point,' by a light *abatis*, which might afford an easy and safe approach to a body of troops."

In accordance with this theory, as shown in the fuller report of Wayne to his superior, on the 17th, two days after the assault, the van of the right, under command of Lieut. Col. Fleury, "preceded by twenty picked men," proceeded to remove the obstructions on the south; the van of the left, under command of Major Stewart, "preceded by a brave and experienced officer, with twenty men," was sent in for the same purpose, viz: "the removal of abatis," on the north side of the hill. Another remark occurring in General Wayne's report confirms this; he says: "At twelve o'clock the assault was to begin on the *right* and *left* of the enemy's works, whilst Major Murfey amused them in front. But a deep morass, covering their whole front, and at this time overflowed by the tide, together with other obstructions, rendered the approaches more difficult than was at first apprehended, so that it was about twenty minutes after twelve before the assault began; previously to which, I placed myself at the head of Febriger's regiment, *on the right* column, and gave the troops most pointed orders not to fire on any account, but place their whole dependence on the bayonet." Neither the deep morass (which surrounds the whole battle ground on the west and south), the formidable and double rows of abatis, nor the strong works in *front* and *flank*, could damp the ardor of the troops, who, in the face of a most tremendous fire of musketry, and from cannon loaded with grape shot, forced their way, at the point of the bayonet, through every obstacle; both columns meeting in the center of the enemy's works nearly at the same instant.

From several well settled facts we are certain that the main attack was from the south. With this part of the army, Wayne and Fleury ascended the hill. (See map.)

The "center" of the enemy's stronghold was undoubtedly in the low, flat surface, and immediately west of the spot where the lighthouse now stands, the entire garrison containing at least two acres of land. (See our cut of the battle.) This place, the lighthouse foundation, which all strangers naturally look upon as the center of the enemy's garrison, was, in our opinion, but the main redoubt for the storage of ammunition, weapons, etc., and occupying the most commanding position, afforded the best view of the entire river, north, east and south. The cannon, which had been placed on eminences to the west of this supposed fort, best commanded an effective range of the enemy's front, facing the "marsh," the "causeway" and the "ravine," across which Wayne had stationed his reserves of three hundred men, under command of General Muhlenburg.

In another part of the same report, Wayne says, "the officers and privates of the artillery *exerted* themselves *in turning the can-*

non against *Verplanck's Point*, and forced the enemy to cut cable of their shipping and run down the river." By this description, it is clear that the cannon must have been in position to sweep the western slope, and if they were to do execution eastward, they must be hauled to a high point to enable them to do effective work on the British ships which were anchored off Verplanck's. Besides, the General commanding, in giving a sketch of the enemy's works, speaks of them as follows: "The sketch herewith transmitted will give you a general idea of the *strength of their works on the west side*, which, in my opinion, are formidable; I think too much so, for a storm; and to attempt to reduce it by regular approaches will require time, as there is *no ground within less distance than half a mile but what it commands*."

The entire front and flanks of the enemy were posted with sentry. Batteries and earthworks were scattered around the entire circle. In his directions as to how to proceed, Gen. Washington especially requested that each commander should know in advance "precisely what batteries or particular parts of the line" they were "respectively to possess," that "confusion and the consequences of indecision" might "be avoided."

An examination of the marsh, "sandy beach," and causeway, convinces one of this. The sentries had been taken, and the skirmishers driven in. Anthony Wayne, at the head of the advance column, had successfully passed the first abatis, and was passing the second when he was wounded in the scalp by a musket ball, and falling to the ground, with considerable effort, in a partly erect posture, shouted: "March on! carry me into the fort, for I will die at the head of my column." Captain Tishbourn and Mr. Archer, his aides-de-camp, supported him while he walked, bleeding and faint, into the works of the enemy.

A general shout from the throats of the dying, the lips of the victors and the entreaties of the vanquished, followed the booming of cannon and the clattering of musketry.

Honorable mention was made by the General in command of the great humanity of the brave soldiers who scorned to take the lives of a vanquished foe calling for mercy, and states that this act reflected the highest honor on them, and accounted for the few of the enemy killed on the occasion.

So high was the excitement that Lieutenant Colonel Fleury struck the British flag with his own hand.

A remarkable fact is recorded, that while the British did all the firing of which they were capable and the Americans did none, the former lost in killed sixty-three men, and the latter but fifteen. The wounded, however, in the American army amounted to eighty-three. The number of the men holding the garrison, and who fell into the hands of the Americans, was about six hundred; while it was the opinion of the Engineer and Washington, and all the officers, who held a subsequent consultation as to the propriety of sustaining the fort, that it would require, at least, fifteen hundred men to make it completely defensible. This is also an additional evidence that the garrison contained at least several acres.

Some allusion is made in the correspondence between Washing and Wayne as to precautions in securing the *Passes* leading to Stony Point. Perhaps there is no word that will as well convey a correct idea of the roughness of the entire country surrounding the famous battle ground. So much of the land as was not heavily timbered was in great part covered, especially on the low grounds, with heavy, tangled undergrowth—alder, thorn and brier. Before its occupancy by troops, Stony Point was seldom visited except by hunters and the wood chopper. King's Ferry was built as a military necessity, the wharf of the commerce of the river being located in the region of the present Penny Bridge.

THE WASHINGTON TREE.

A dozen houses would constitute the entire community. On the old Erskine map, six houses or buildings are shown—DeNoyelle's, Benson's, W. Smith's (The Treason House,) a house at the fork of the road near the "Washington Tree," of which we have an engraving, Flora Krom, on the east slope of Kalebergh Mountain, a blacksmith shop at the corner where R. B. Marks' store is located and King's Ferry. These are land marks; others, no doubt, existed.

Our chapter on the "Traditions of the Revolution" will describe some of them.

We add the following interesting quotations from the *Magazine* of the metropolitan publishing house, Harper Bros., dated the year of the centennial of the capture: "The struggle of the Revolution in reality, centered here. No strategic position any where in the thirteen colonies was more eagerly coveted on the one side or more sleeplessly watched on the other, than these same Highlands. They formed, as it were, the covered way between the strong New England section and the rest of the States to the southward, by which they all kept their chain of communication, sympathy and mutual assistance unbroken. It was to capture and occupy this position that Burgoyne marched down with his formidable expedition from Canada, through the Horicon (silvery water), as named by Fenimore Cooper, and now known as Lake George; and it was for the same purpose that that infamous plot of treachery and desertion was concocted between Arnold and Sir Henry Clinton, in 1780. Throughout the long struggle the region was never for a moment bared of defences. Here fortifications had been commenced as early as 1775; here troops marched and countermarched in every campaign; and here on the Hudson lay the last cantonment of the army of the Revolution when the soldiers were dismissed to their homes at the close of the war."

THE CAPTURE OF STONY POINT. 41

RIVER VIEW.

Referring to the scene of the capture the same writer continues: "Stony Point, a bold, rocky peninsular, 200 feet high at its summit, juts out far into the river; and when the water does not surround its base, a marsh seems to isolate it from the main. Verplanck's, nearly opposite, slightly above, having not half this height, nevertheless has a commanding range. Irving calls these promontories "the lower gates of the Highlands, or miniature Pillars of Hercules, of which Stony Point is the Gibraltar."

CHAPTER VI.

THE FORGOTTEN MONUMENTS OF OUR HEROES.

COULD the everlasting hills and the granite peaks of our historic river break the silence of a century, they would speak of the deeds of the brave patriots; but their silence will never break; they will wait for other tongues:

"Mark—on the Highlands' frieze, the noted train,
　The victors' marshalled triumph, throng
In bold procession to Liberty's fane,
　With many a federal symbol move along.
Lone are thy pillars now; each gale
　Sighs over them as a spirit's voice which moaned
That loneliness, and told the plaintive tale
　Of the bright Campus by Continentals owned.
Weep, cherished ruins! parched on Highland Hill,
　Thy peers in other lands have shared
The same neglect, and standing still,
　That wasting elements have yet in mercy spared.
Each commemorative mark by valor made,
　Will treasures of patriotic love be laid.
Yes; in those fragments—those by time defaced,
　And rude, insensate conquerers—yet remains
All that may charm the enlightened eye of taste

>On shores where still inspiring freedom reigns.
>As vital fragrance breathes from every part
>>Of the crushed myrtle, or the bruised rose—
>E'en thus the essential of art,
>>There in each wreck imperishably glows.
>The soul of Washington lives in every line,
>Pervading brightly still the spirit of his time."

Temples of religions antiquated, towers of human ambition, have mouldered to dust; images of savage nations have fallen to the earth; but why should those fortresses of our Revolutionary achievement be allowed to level to the earth and be overgrown by forests, or fall into the oblivion of the ordinary furrows of the field, and be looked for in vain and with sadness by the sons of our patriot dead? On many—yes, sadly many—a spot where fell the martyrs of our freedom, some to rise no more, others to bear their honorable scars to future graves, not a common stone of the great multitude on the ground, is reared. The poet has pictured never so truly and vividly of these as in the following words:

>"The thousands that, uncheered by praise,
>Have made one offering of their days
>For Truth, for Heaven, for Freedom's sake—
>Resigned, the bitter cup to take;
>And silently, in fearless faith,
>Bowing their noble souls to death.
>Where sleep they, Earth? By no proud stone
>Their narrow couch of rest is known.
>The still sad glory of their name,
>Hallows no mountain unto Fame;
>No; not a tree the record bears,
>Of their deep thoughts and lonely prayers."

True; of the spot where a hundred brave men fell before an equal number of the foe, some to rise no more, not even a stone, of the many available on that rocky promontory, has chiseled upon its face the important event. With what patriot pride and solemn emotion would our grateful people, whose pilgrimages to these sacred grounds are annually increasing, look upon such a worthy shrine of American devotion!

Standing, a few days ago, on the same old ground once pressed by our intrepid, assaulting patriots, we were overcome by the emotion of the hour. The following poem rose in beautiful silence, but awful meaning:

> "O, that the many rustling leaves,
> Which round our homes the summer weaves,
> Or that the stream, in whose glad voice
> Our own familiar paths rejoice,
> Might whisper through the starry sky
> To tell where these blest slumberers lie;
> But the old woods and sounding waves
> Are silent of those hidden graves."

No spot on the wide field, over which the Revolutionary fathers fought, is of greater historic interest, or more deserving of national fame or monumental marking, than these consecrated Stony Point battle grounds; and yet we question, prompted by patriotism, that no spot of land of similar fame, has fewer visitors to mourn at its shrine or plant an ivy against the rugged rocks. While many do come, many more would come if the Government grounds were made more intelligible and inviting. Then the thousands from our cities, and the multitudes that pass by on the steamers, and tens of thousands that speed by on the Expresses of the great West Shore Railroad, would feel induced to halt for a few hours and ramble among the scenes made precious by the daring and sacrifice of our patriot dead. Children would come with songs

"To bless the band,
Amidst whose mossy graves we stand."

In the absence of man's monument to the departed, the gray, bald rocks like sentinels are still there.

"They saw the princely crest,
They saw the kingly spear,
The banner and the mail-clad breast
Borne down and trampled here.
They saw; and glorying there they stand
Eternal records to the land.

Long—even a whole century—the bold rocks have kept intact and bared the foundations for the projected "Wayne Monument," which our tender and grateful Republic are to rear upon. It was a matter of pride and joy that our lamented Congressman, Beach, had so nearly secured the national appropriation of $25,000 for its erection. We hope that his worthy successor, Hon. Henry Bacon, will, by all lawful means, fulfill the wishes of our people. May we not confidently indulge in the hope that with the ushering in of the Monumental Age this most worthy, yet hitherto unhonored spot, may yet be immortalized by enduring and polished granite, that the traveler passing by may remember that on yonder promontory our fathers fought for our common liberty?

CHAPTER VII.

THE TREASON OF ARNOLD.

BY C. B. STORY.

YOU will not fail me now! On to the fortress, my brave soldiers, you and you, on again! You know me well. Such were the words that rang out amidst the din of battle, October 7, 1777. A black horse and rider are seen pushing forward through the smoke and shot from a thousand guns, and Benedict Arnold is carried bleeding and wounded from the field, shouting, "The Battle is ours! Saratoga is won!"

If the shadowy curtains of life had then closed over that bleeding form and some good angel borne away that heroic spirit, the darkest chapter in the annals of our American Revolution would never have been written. But the mystery of human destiny is great, and often beyond the control of man.

In the following pages the writer will endeavor to give a plain and trustworthy account of that painful event, so intimately associated with the scenes around us.

Benedict Arnold was born at Norwich, Conn., on the third day of January, 1740. His early life, like that of most boys, was uneventful until his enlistment in the army, when 16 years of age. In March, 1775, he was chosen the head of a body of troops. He went to Cambridge, and while there proposed to go and capture Ticonderoga and Crown Point. On the way he overtook Ethan Allen; and together they took the above named forts, also St. John's. In the same Autumn he was put in command of 1200 men with instructions to ascend the Kennebec and Chandice rivers, and thence to attack Quebec. He marched to the plains of Abraham, but was not strong enough to be successful, even with Montgomery's help.

In July, 1777, he joined the army under Schuyler, and engaged in the battle of Saratoga, there showing that extraordinary daring recorded at the beginning of this article. After this he resigned his command under General Gates, came to Albany, and while there, on account of his great bravery, was commissioned a Major General, dated back.

His wounds being sufficiently healed, he proceeded to Valley Forge, in May of the following Spring, and again joined the army. Washington gave him the command of Philadelphia, which city had lately been evacuated by the British.

It was during this command, that his manner of living became extravagant, and his business affairs complicated. For a short time he lived a wild and dissipated life, and, under apprehension of charges, resigned his command, and a Court Martial soon followed, Washington reprimanding him for his conduct. He felt the injury of this keenly, and probably at this time the infamous plot of treason began to take root in his mind.

During his command in the city, he had met with a beautiful and accomplished Tory lady, to whom he joined himself in marriage. His wife being an intimate friend of John Andre, Brigadier General of the British army, under Sir Henry Clinton, the way now seemed opened whereby his scheme of treachery could be carried out. For some time a correspondence was carried on between Arnold and Clinton through the means of Andre, each of them assuming a fictitious name, and thus concealing their identity.

The treason was not long in gaining serious proportions. Arnold applied to Washington for the command of West Point, on the Hudson, which was then the strongest post in the American lines, it being a bond between the Eastern and Middle

Colonies and containing the supply of ammunition for the whole army.

Arnold took up his headquarters at the house of Beverly Robinson, now known as the "Robinson House," about two and one half miles south from West Point, on the east side of the river. Everything was now in readiness for the final transactions and for consummation of the plot. A personal interview only seemed necessary for its completion. This was arranged to take place between Andre and Arnold, Andre having been selected for the purpose by Sir Henry Clinton.

The question now presented itself, where shall the meeting take place? Several places seem to have been thought of, but that of Dobb's Ferry was given precedence, that being neutral ground. The meeting was to take place on the night of September 11th. Arnold accordingly left the "Robinson House," and pro-

RESIDENCE OF J. H. SMITH, 1770.
TREASON HOUSE

ceeding down the river, crossed at King's Ferry (which at that time afforded passage between Verplanck's and Stony Point,) and thence over the King's Highway toward Haverstraw. The night of the 10th he spent at the house of J. H. Smith, now known as the "Treason House," occupied by E. B. Weiant, and owned by B. J. Allison. The next day he pushed on to the place appointed for the meeting.

The British man-of-war "Vulture" had come up the river, and anchored near this place. The meeting, however, did not take place as was expected, and Arnold returned to his headquarters at the Robinson House.

He again made arrangements to meet on the night of the 20th, promising to send a messenger on board the Vulture, who

STAIRWAY IN THE TREASON HOUSE.

would conduct Andre, under a flag of truce, to a place of safety on shore.

In the meantime the Vulture had received orders to proceed up as far as Teller's Point, nearly opposite to Haverstraw. Arnold came down again, went to the Smith House, and engaged J. H. Smith to meet Andre, and bring him on shore. Smith did as directed, and in the still hours of night landed him in a lonely spot at the base of the mountains, just below Haverstraw, near what is known as Long Clove. Arnold was there to meet him, and silently they crept away into the bushes. Hour after hour passed away until Smith and his boatmen, weary of waiting, told them they must leave, as it was nearing daybreak. Their plans were not yet completed, so the boatmen were ordered to return, and Arnold, with Andre, went up to the Smith House, there to complete their secret work. While engaged in their business, sitting at a table in an upper room, they were suddenly startled by the booming of a cannon. Andre ran to the window, which commands a full view of the river in the direction where the Vulture had lain. After the firing Andre returned to the table, and they renewed their work. The Vulture dropped down the river. All this, while Andre had doubtless entertained the hope of making his way back to the boat from which the Smith crew had brought him. Meantime, Smith saw the situation, and refused to conduct Andre back to the sloop; whereupon, the unfortunate spy resolved upon a return to the British lines by land. Arnold had taken his leave of him, and having furnished him with a proper pass, supposed, of course, he would have no trouble to return. Just before evening, on the 22d, Andre, accompanied by Smith, who had loaned him a suit of his citizens' clothes, started up for King's Ferry, where he crossed. They rode until nine o'clock in the evening, and put up at the house of one Andrew Miller. Early the next morning he was on his way to New York, and had arrived within a few miles of the British lines, when he was confronted by three men. The capture is best told in the words of the men themselves. Mr. Sparks quotes them as follows:

"Myself" said Paulding, "Isaac Van Wart, and David Williams, were lying by the side of the road, about half a mile above Tarrytown, and about fifteen miles above Kingsbridge, on Saturday morning, between nine and ten o'clock, the 23d of September. We had laid there about one hour and a half, as near as I can recollect, and saw several persons we were acquainted with, whom we let pass. Presently, one of the young men who was with me, said, 'There comes a gentleman-like looking man, who appears to be well dressed, and has boots on, and whom you had better step out and stop, if you dont know him.' On that, I got up and presented my firelock at the breast of the person, and told him to stand; and then I asked him which way he was going. 'Gentlemen,' said he, 'I hope you belong to our party.' I asked him what party. He said 'The Lower Party.' Upon that, I told him I did; then he said, 'I am a British officer out in this country on particular business, and I hope you will not detain me a minute;' and to show that he was a British officer, he pulled out his watch; upon which I told him to dismount. He then said, 'My God! I must do anything to get along!' and seemed to make a kind of laugh of it, and pulled out General Arnold's pass, which was to John Anderson, to pass all guards to White Plains and below. Upon this he dismounted. Said he: 'Gentlemen, you had best let me go, or you will get yourselves into trouble, for your stopping me will detain the General's business;' and said he was going to Dobb's Ferry to meet a person there and get intelligence for General Arnold. Upon that I told him I hoped he would not be offended; that we did not mean to take anything from him; and I told him there were many bad people on the road, and I did not know but perhaps he might be one."

"We took him into the bushes," said Williams, "and ordered him to pull off his clothes, which he did; but on searching him narrowly we could not find any sort of writings. We told him to pull off his boots, which he seemed to be indifferent about; but we got one boot off, and searched in that boot, and could find nothing; but we found there were some papers in the bottom of his stocking, next to his foot, on which we made him pull his stocking off, and found three papers wrapped up. Mr. Paulding looked at the contents, and said he was a spy. We then made him pull off his other boot, and there found three more papers at the bottom of his foot, within his stocking. Upon this we made him dress himself, and I asked him what he would give us to let him go. He said he would give us any sum of money. I asked him whether he would give us his horse, saddle, bridle, watch and one hundred guineas. He said 'yes,' and told us he would direct them to any place, even if it was that very spot, so that we could get them. I asked him whether he would not give us more. He said he would give us any quantity of dry goods or any sum of money, and bring it to any place we might pitch upon, so that we might get it. Mr. Paulding answered 'No; if you would give us ten thousand guineas, you should not stir one step.' I then asked the person, who called himself John Anderson, if he would not get away if it lay in his power. He answered, 'Yes; I would.' I told him I did not intend he should. While taking him along we asked him a few questions, and we stopped under a shade. He begged us not to ask him questions, and said when he came to any commander he would reveal all."

The three men, with their captive, proceeded to the nearest military post, which was at North Castle. Colonel Jameson, the commander in charge, examined the papers of the prisoner, and at once pronounced him a spy. Not believing Arnold implicated in the treachery, although the papers were signed by his name, he immediately ordered him sent to Arnold's headquarters, which order, however, was countermanded by Major Tallmadge, and the prisoner taken to Lower Salem. Arnold was at breakfast when the news arrived that Andre had been taken prisoner. He excused himself without emotion, called his wife aside, and in a few words told her of his danger. She fell at his feet in a swoon, but without hesitation, he quickly left the scene, hurried to the river where his boat was moored, and ordered his men to row him to the Vulture, promising them a good allowance of whiskey for their extra efforts.

Washington had just returned from the east, and was inspecting the works along the river when the traitor made his flight. On crossing to West Point a little later in the day, Hamilton met him and told him all. Washington feared the worst, but with remarkable self-possession, gave orders that every possible precaution be taken to prevent an attack.

Instruction was given that Andre should be sent to the Robinson House, and the next day, September 28th, he was sent from there down to Tappan. Washington followed, and the next day ordered a hearing of Andre's case before several general officers. Their report was as follows: "That Major John Andre, Adjutant General of the British army, ought to be considered as a spy from the enemy; and that, agreeably to the laws and usage of nations, it is their opinion he ought to suffer death." The sentence was approved by Washington, and Andre sentenced to be hanged October 2d, at 12 m., which sentence was executed at the appointed hour.

Arnold accepted an office in the British army, and about $50,000, for his treason. He afterward went to England, and there lived out a miserable existence, "Arnold, the Traitor" having become a name despised on both continents.

The treason of Arnold was a most dastardly attempt to ruin

the hopes of the American army, but, on the whole, really contributed to its fidelity and strength.

The "Treason House" still stands on yonder "Treason Hill," and the record given in these pages shows its historical association.

CHAPTER VIII.

OPERATIONS ON THE HUDSON.

MR. J. COE, writing to Gen. Washington under date of "Haverstraw, July 16, 1776," says:

"In consequence of Your Excellency's desire to receive timely information of every manœuvre which the enemy on Hudson's River may make, to distress the inhabitants at this extremely busy season, we can inform Your Excellency that this morning, between the hours of ten and eleven, the whole fleet, consisting of two men-of-war and three tenders, made sail from Nyack, and at about twelve, came into Haverstraw Bay, forty miles up the river from New York, when, after the shipping came to anchor, the tenders continued parading the bay half an hour. They all came to anchor opposite the house of Captain Thiers, when four barges, fully manned, attempted to land with a view, as we conjecture, to take off some sheep and cattle which we had previously driven off. Notwithstanding, they brought their tenders so nigh the shore as to cover the landing of the men in the barges, yet, having but a few men, we savored a firm countenance to them, and with a few shot, being well leveled, they thought proper to retreat, without doing any damage with their cannon."

Gen. Hays, writing to Washington under date of "July 19, 1776," said:

"The enemy now lie in Haverstraw Bay, and are using every effort to land and destroy the property of the inhabitants. The great extent of shore I have to guard obliges me to keep the greatest part of my regiment on duty, in order to prevent their depredations. I have received a reinforcement from Gen. Clinton, at Fort Montgomery, of about 80 men, and hope when he receives Your Excellency's letter he will send me further relief, as the enemy seem to direct their operations against the west shore. We are in want of powder and ball. If I had two or three small cannon I should have been able to have destroyed one of the cutters that grounded near Stony Point, and laid there six hours."

On the "17th of July, 1776," in a letter by Washington to Congress, the following occurs:

"They were sounding the water up towards the Highlands, by which, it is probable, they will attempt to pass with part of their fleet, if possible."

Of the men raised for the defense of the shore, Col Hays writes in a letter to his Chief as follows:

"My regiment consists of but 400 men, one-fourth of whom, with eighty men sent me by Gen. Clinton, I find necessary to keep on constant duty. This precinct has already raised two companies for the Continental service. The vicinity of the mountains, being poor, is thinly inhabited, by people of small estates. This, together with the great extent of shore we have to guard, is extremely burdensome to the people, and, I suppose, is the true reason that has induced Captain Parker (of the British) to fix his station in Haverstraw Bay."

Gen. Greene writes Gen. Washington from King's Ferry, Nov. 5, 1776. In that letter he speaks of using boats to transport flour from Dobb's Ferry to Peekskill, and that there were sufficient troops along the shore to protect the passage of vessels up the river. The King's Ferry was a prominent point. Its water front was most advantageous on account of its abrupt and yet sandy shore. Gen. Sterling speaks of it under date of Nov. 10, 1776. He found landing on the coast (probably of Grassy Point) very difficult, " as at half tide the vessels are obliged to lay at the distance of five or six hundred yards from the shore, which makes tedious work with the few boats that are here; besides, it is open to any insult the enemy is pleased to commit. About *half a mile further north and on the north side of Stony Point, is a good landing place in deep water, and easily secured* by placing two cannon on the end of the point. It will require about half a mile of new road, a short causeway and a small bridge." From the foregoing description, we infer that King's Ferry was, at an earlier day, lower down the river. As it was before it could not have been protected by cannon; this is one reason for its removal further north. Mention is made of its being desirable to move it one-half mile farther north. It may be that two landings were used, and according to present appearances this was so.

The military operations in this section undoubtedly gave great significance to the Ferry; but it must also be borne in mind that all communication between the opposite sides of the Hudson had to be carried on by boats. The names of boats used at that early date give us some idea of their construction. They were barges, schooners, sloops, brigs, galleys, lighters, flat boats, pontoons, traders, etc.

In one of Gen. Heath's Orders of Nov. 17, 1776, he says: " Sir, You will repair with your detachment and boats to King's Ferry, where you will remain until further orders. You will order your boatmen to ferry over the Hudson river all such officers and soldiers belonging to the army of the United States of America, as may from time to time have orders or permission to pass the river, and also all horses, wagons and baggage belonging to the Army. . . You will also observe such directions as have been given in charge to the officer whom you relieve."

Colonel Hays dates a letter from King's Ferry on the 25th day of November, 1776. The Colonel had a landing of his own, but it was on the Minnesceecongo Creek at the foot of the lane on his farm, and in order to get to the Hudson by row boat must follow the winding stream to its outlet at the end of the "farther neck," as Grassy Point was then called. Undoubtedly many years prior to the Revolution a landing at the mouth of the Minnesceecongo was used for shipping purposes. It was, until the erection of the N. J. & N. Y. Railway and the West Shore Railway, the only way of travel except when the river was frozen up, at which time the very infrequent journeys to New York City were by private conveyance and public stage. But "Hay's landing" was also on the river lower down in Haverstraw. As Gen. Lee writes to Gen. Heath, Dec. 4, 1776:

"Sir, The troops here are so distressed for rum this rainy weather that I must request you'll immediately forward ten hogsheads of rum down to Colonel Hay's landing in Haverstraw."

An interesting social event took place. A vessel, under flag of truce, came up in the interest of a Rev. Mr. Inglis and one Mr. Moore in search of their respective families, who had been left in the vicinity of Peekskill, but Gen. Heath, shrewd and cautious, stopped the vessel just opposite our place. Row boats were kept moving round the schooner all night; and not until an order reached the General from the Commander-in-Chief, who was then at the convention in Trenton, would the distinguished reverend and his friend be allowed to pass.

The difficulties with which the brave Gen. Hawkes Hays, who was defending these shores and his native homestead, were surrounded, are set forth in the following quotation: " Yesterday afternoon I received your order to send down to Tappan 30 barrels of flour, and to Paramus 80 barrels of flour and thirty barrels of pork. I have myself, and two hands that I hired, been out all night, and cannot get any teams to convey the flour to Paramus. All the wagons and horses are already in the service with General Lee. We found a few ox teams, but their owners will not let them go, and I have nobody here to take them away by force. I am at a loss what to do. I must beg your advice in this affair. As for pork, I have none. If you want beef, I can send you plenty of that article. This day Captain Hyatt set out to Paramus with a drove of cattle.—A. Hawkes Hay."

This natural opening of country between the Palisade and the Highlands seems, by nature, to have been fitted for an important arena of the great Revolution.

All the important movements from the northern and from the southern sections seem to have moved like a mighty trail of battalions for the long eight years of the bloody struggle. Mt. " Thor," on the south, gazed often on the surging troops of the opposing forces, on what seemed sometimes to be neutral ground ; while the belching cannon of West Point, Fort Montgomery, Fort Clinton, Fort Independence, Dunderburg, Verplanck and Stony Point drove fear, fire and death into the ascending fleets of the King.

Great military stores and ammunition were at times housed and guarded between the passes of these gigantic arms of the mountains which surround us.

Andre, the spy, saw our shore to covet it, but passed over it for the last time on the errand to his execution at Tappan.

In an order dated at Newburg, April 18, 1783, the Commander-in-Chief uses the following beautiful language:

"While the General recollects the almost infinite variety of scenes through which we have passed with a mixture of pleasure, astonishment and gratitude; while he contemplates the prospect before us with rapture, he cannot help wishing that all the brave men (of whatever condition they be) who have shared in the toils and dangers of effecting this glorious revolution, of rescuing millions from the hand of oppression, and of laying the foundation of a great empire, might be impressed with a proper idea of the dignified part they have been called to act (under the smiles of Providence) on the stage of human affairs. For happy, thrice happy, shall they be pronounced hereafter who have contributed anything, who have performed the meanest office in erecting this stupendous fabric of freedom and empire on the broad basis of independency; who have assisted in protecting the rights of human nature and establishing an asylum for the poor and oppressed of all nations and religions."

These same shores which, in the first period of the Revolution, witnessed the going out of volunteers to prescribe a dubious war, were the first to hear the tramp of "*veteran soldiers*, covered with laurels, returning from the field to their peaceful abodes."

CHAPTER IX.

TRADITIONS OF THE REVOLUTION.

THE following chapter is traditional, and is published as a feature of the work for just what it is said to be. The statements contained in the chapter are reliable, as they relate to what old people have said. Their sayings are interesting reading for the young, and awaken in such a taste for the study of history.

There are persons still living here who heard their ancestors speak of the great sufferings of the soldiers, and that citizens had bound up their feet, which had become sore from excessive marching and exposure.

Mr. Samuel Goetchius, over eighty years of age, recollects hearing an old lady describe the fear the people were in during those dark days.

He was acquainted, when a young man, with a Revolutionary soldier by the name of Frank Sayres, and says that he lived with his son, Abraham Sayres. He knew another man by name of Capt. Wm. Conklin. His wife survived him, and lived for many years where Jas. Keesler now resides. She drew a pension during her widowhood. She often spoke of having been driven into the woods for the protection of herself and her five children. She lies buried opposite the Potter's field on the Lowland Hill.

The grandfather of Samuel Goetchius was about eighteen years old during the war, and drove team in the Revolution. This same man relates that he was well acquainted with Aunt Polly James, who lived near "Buckleburgh." She heard the firing of the fort, and visited the grounds afterwards. She related that the Americans, on capturing the place at night, turned the guns upon the enemy, whose ships were anchored off Verplancks.

Tradition says that a few days before the final assault of the fort, detailed soldiers went about from house to house and destroyed the dogs, so as to compel the utmost secrecy and quietness, in view of the expected surprise.

The place known as "Crickettown" had a resident family who was visited by a squad of soldiers and asked to deliver up their dog on the evening before the assault.

G. B. Weiant, sixty-five years of age, distinctly recollects when young helping to pull down the old John Crom House, which stood immediately south of the Washington Tree. Though probably an inferior house, yet it was important enough to be marked on the map made by an engineer in the Revolution.

Several previous histories have made allusion to the large walnut tree under which it is said Washington halted his troops during a march over the King's Highway, and that he had here made a payment to his men. That the tree as shown in our cut is the same tree that stood there then there is no reason to doubt. We have known trees in our youth that were very large and had very ancient records as monuments of land surveys. Pear trees have been known to attain the age of two hundred years. Many of the forest trees on our native hills would have marked two centuries if not cruelly cut down by the axe of the lumberman.

The walnut tree we are writing of was formerly surrounded by a small grove of the same species. A mammoth one was cut down some years ago. Its logs were drawn to Esquire Beebe's saw mill, which was located near John A. Bulson's store, and con-

verted into lumber for the manufacture of gun stocks, canes and altar rails. The chancel rail now used in St. George's M. E. Church is said to have been worked out of the above-named lumber.

Major Adam Lilburn, a man of large estate and unusual public spirit, has recently expended a considerable amount of labor on the grounds surrounding the Washington Tree. The old meadow has undergone thorough renovation, the soil cleared of stone, uneven places leveled, all trees, except the " sacred" one, removed. A strong wall encloses the lot along the highway. The farm immediately in front of the Treason House was once the possession of Colonel Hawkes Hay, an officer of great distinction in the military operations along the shores of the Hudson.

The veritable " lane " running easterly to the landing on the bank of the Minnescecongo Creek is still kept intact. We have often driven over the very drive. A stone wall closes the entrance now.

The Treason House, as originally built, was a square stone building, rather well built. The father of the Smiths was Wm. Smith, a judge of the courts. They were a family of somewhat aristocratic notions, and were not particularly popular as neighbors. Feuds were avoided, but during the dark days of the Revolution they were not in active sympathy with the cause of American Independence. The residence of Joseph Hette Smith, on account of the meeting there of Arnold and Andre, has gone into history under the title of the " Treason House." It is owned by B. J. Allison, and is occupied as a summer boarding house by the painter and grainer, E. B. Weiant.

Flora Falls, whose clear waters pour over the red bank opposite the homestead of Mr. B. J. Allison, were originally named Florus Falls, from the incident of their source on the farm of

THOMAS DINAN'S HOUSE, GRASSY POINT.

Florus Crown. The village of Stony Point was known as Flora Falls. It long went by the name of Knight's Corner, on account of the store kept here formerly by Wm. Knight.

Formerly our town was embraced in the Land Patent obtained by grant from Phillip Carterett, Esq., who was in 1664 one of the owners of "New Cesarea," as New Jersey was then called. The title for this portion of the grant was secured by Beltazar De Hart.

Some curious names then existed, of which the following are samples: Caquuaney, Newasink, Menisakeungu, Averstraw, Yandakah, Aquamek and Haverstroo.

Fifty years ago there stood a pretentious house on the bluff near the low point of land in the neighborhood of the Diamond Brick Yards, at which point the Minnesecongo Creek runs very close to the Hudson, as though it once sought an outlet at that point. This mansion, which had few superiors on the Hudson, was known as "Rosa Villa," on account of the profusion of flowers growing about the house. The next house of note was that built by Dr. Proudfoot at Grassy Point landing in 1830, although an earlier one had been erected by the Dennings. All these houses were well built for their day. The one now occupied by Thomas Dinan is a fair specimen, having been then erected. It is engraved for this volume.

The colored man, Pompey, whom the traditions honor with the great feat of having led the vanguard of Wayne's men to the enemy's picket, must have widened out considerably on that occasion to have been able to serve as a personal guide to three attacking columns at one time. The wonderful story of the achievement of the great Pompey has never grown less, but with each repetition it seems that new lustre has been added. Very clever traditions say he was put in command of a company of infantry, and was splendidly uniformed, by way of special distinction. It is said that while Pompey was chatting with the British sentinel, the latter was suddenly seized by the men whom the guide had brought with him. This may or may not be the order of things; but would it not be more in keeping with the circumstances to say that Pompey's chief services on the occasion were in the fact of his having, by special agreement, procured the countersign for the Americans on the evening of the attack. This was one of the chief purposes of the reconnoitre in the early part of the night— and for which purpose other guides had been secured—while the troops were halting at Springsteels, from which place Wayne wrote his brother-in-law just "before the columns moved forward." Up to this hour, 11 o'clock p. m., 15th July, few, if any, of the hundreds of privates of Wayne's army had been apprised of the work before them. Every citizen in the vicinity of Stony Point had been secured, either as a guide to lead the "twenty picked men," or put under guard to prevent their desertion to the enemy. We venture the opinion that Pompey did little effective service beyond giving the password for that night, and that on the discharge of the first gun, and that, too, on the outside of *the first row of abatis*, Pompey retired with accelerated speed.

According to an English plan of the garrison, there were seven picket stations, perched on as many hills, on the outside of the first row of abatis. It is natural to suppose that if the works were so "formidable," that a perfect line of pickets extended all the way round the grounds lying east of the morass which surrounds the entire promontory, from the King's Road, which crosses the "Mud Bridge" near the ascent of hill, as one would go up toward Dr. N. Garrison's. The entire grounds of the promontory, as clearly described by our accompanying map, are fully a half mile in length, and according to all traditions it was at this "Mud Bridge" that some portion of Wayne's men crossed. When the tide is at flood, especially at very high tide, the marsh is entirely overflowed, making the promontory literally an island, though the marsh is fast becoming a peaty meadow.

Mr. John Ten Eyck, who lives on the adjoining high grounds, says he has many times rowed a boat around the point.

If Pompey was the slave of Mr. Lamb, whose residence at that time stood on the high ground which formerly extended out as far as the locality of the present store of D. Tompkins & Sons, it would be natural to suppose that, in making his market visits to the British garrison, he would take the causeway leading directly from his "massa's" house to the foot of the hill, where the first abatis cornered. The first line of abatis, according to the map, was about in the neighborhood of the residence of Miles Duffney, or a little to the east of this house. The troops themselves needed this causeway to get to their "Day Picket" this side the morass, (See map). If the right column, before which Wayne says he had placed himself, "did not cross over this causeway, they were as likely to have come along and descended" the eastern slope of the high ground, north of the "Green House," now occupied by Charles Casseles, and to have waded the narrow part of the marsh on the west side of the present West Shore Railroad, as to have forded the Bay, as indicated by the dotted lines on the King's map. Tradition says they passed immediately north of, and close by, Duffney's house. For Wayne to have passed the first, and to have been wounded while passing the second abatis, we cannot see that any other route was feasible. The enemy may have made a mistake as to the exact spot where the Americans ascended, as the column was spread, immediately after its entrance, through the opening made by the twenty picked men who preceded them. Such was the general excitement all along the line, from the extreme north side of the hill, where Major Stewart was at work, to the front, (that is the west) where Major Murfey was "amusing them," round the south side or "right flank," where Col. Fleury was advancing through the abatis, that it might be fair to assume that the rush of men, who forced their way, at the point of the bayonet, through every obstacle, both columns meeting in the center of the enemy's works nearly at the same instant, left it a matter of much uncertainty as to the precise spot where the right and left columns met in the "center of the enemy's works." The map, showing the abatis and position of the troops, was, no doubt, drawn at the leisure of the British Engineer before the assault, and was tolerably correct, though found to be otherwise by a careful survey of the point, by Prof. L. Wilson, who took advantage of the ice on the river in getting his bearings. According to the British outlines of Wayne's assault, the Americans simply surrounded the hill, but Wayne's account of it makes him pass through the *two rows of abatis*, and that the men gained the works "in the face of a most tremendous fire of musketry," and "cannon loaded with grape shot."

Tradition says the dead were buried about in the locality in which they fell. The burial plot pointed out is near the corner of the outer abatis, on the south side of the hill. It is a remarkable fact, too, that the cannon were mainly located and pointed in this direction. Here was the "8-inch Howitzer," the "24" and "18-pounder ship guns," one "iron 12-pounder," also the short "brass 12-pounder," which covered the lower corner of the first abatis, and according to all this array of cannon, the center of the British works must have been considerably west of the present site of the lighthouse, which would comport very well with Wayne's description of the surprise. Besides all this, the capture occurred at midnight—too dark for close observation as to the directions the Americans came and spread.

It is barely possible, too, that the King's geographer did not like to give too minute a description so early as March 1st, 1781. Things were a little unsettled yet at that time.

Tradition speaks of iron and wooden pins being found in the earth at the causeway in and about the locality we have been describing, and that a certain teamster, many years ago, got his team entangled and seriously injured by getting them in contact with these old abatis.

The balls forming an initial letter in this volume were found by Mr. Watson Tompkins in the vicinity where the above directed cannon could easily have lodged them. The missiles had been deeply imbedded in the clay. It is the only occasion we call up when guns on the redoubts above indicated did any execution in the direction named. Mr. B. J. Allison has balls that were found on the high ground back of his house. This spot is in the direction the cannon pointed. Tradition says that the next day the ground was strewed with the dead. About one hundred lives were lost in the aggregate. Undoubtedly they all sleep on the promontory somewhere. It is but a few years ago that Jacob Rose, father of Isaac Rose, lived to relate the scene of the slain as he witnessed them. He was at that time about twelve years of age, and accompanied his father to the battle ground on the day following the assault, and carried away a musket, hiding it under a log for subsequent use in the defense of his country. Mr. Jas. Knapp, of Western New York, remembers hearing his grandmother say that she visited the camp to minister to the wounded the day following the surrender. She spoke of the fine personal appearance of many of the slain British. The British map speaks of sixty loyal Americans having been stationed at No. 3. That breastwork lies nearest the point where the victorious Americans met in the "enemy's works." It is altogether likely that many of these "loyal" ones were among the unfortunate captives, and that the ministrations alluded to were to relatives of the people now living here. Before the Revolution, the Colonists who were unmindful of King James' orders, and were not willing to be taxed without having some voice in the matter, were called " Rebels." Those same persons afterwards became the true Americans, and the " loyal " ones became the " Tories " or " Rebels." It was according to the teachings of the early ministers, Whitefield, Wesley and other pioneers, that prayers should be offered for the King. Not to be loyal was to be a rebel against the King. So matters stood. It was brother against brother. It is even at this late day unkind and unprincipled to make allusion to families that were " Tories," as though it had been an unmanly principle to be loyal, and yet, such was the sudden crystalization of society into true Americanism, that before the departure of the first generation after the Revolution the odium of having been a Loyalist no longer attached to citizenship, on account of the mere incident of birthright and education, which to this day account for nearly all political and denominational differences. It requires superior intelligence and moral principle to elevate one's self above these mere incidents of life, and every person of good principle will cheerfully forgive all unpatriotic conduct of our forefathers relating to the Revolution.

Around the immortal rocky island of Stony Point Redoubt, more than a century ago, sailed the fleets of our patriot fathers as they bore up under the shadows of " Dunderberg " and hid among the peaks of the Highland range. These picturesque and classic views were the peculiar charm of all the American soldiery of the past. Among the modern warriors none expressed more admiration of our Grand Military Garrison than Generals Kilpatrick and U. S. Grant. The former was more than typified by Mad Anthony Wayne, the latter by the immortal Washington. How tender the nation's regard that these cherished warriors should sleep on the banks of the Revolutionary Hudson!

Montaigne's verses on retirement are appropriate :

> "May Tiber's walls, the Argean Seat,
>   Afford my age a calm retreat!
>   There worn with journeyings, wars and seas,
>   May I enjoy unenvied ease."

General Judson Kilpatrick was a native of Deckertown, N. J., and was for some time neighbor to the writer. A handsome farm on which the General lived before the Rebellion, and to which he retired at its close, is still known as the Kilpatrick Farm. The remains of the General were brought from Chili (where he died in the Government service) during the month of October, 1887, and buried in the Soldiers' Cemetery, West Point. The pall bearers, honored with the tender trust of bearing the body at the burial, were Sergeants Jas. O'Niel, T. Murphy, J. H. Hooker, J. Bayle, James McAuliffe and Corporal J. E. Leonard. From the station to the grave the body was borne on a caisson drawn by six horses. Several Grand Army Posts and a number of distinguished civic and military persons attended. Three volleys were fired over his grave by a battalion of soldiers.

His bold and noble form will no more pass by with its accustomed military salute before these sacred grounds of Anthony Wayne, whom he loved to emulate.

He was buried with the honors and ritual of the Grand Army of the Republic, and afterwards the Catholic priest pronounced the burial service of the Roman Catholic Church, in honor, probably, of the lamented General's wife, who was a Spanish Catholic. The great chief himself, we regret to record, was not religious, yet a braver man nor more loyal soldier never entered the field or drew sabre.

A touching incident concerning the old "charger" which the General rode while in the army we cheerfully and tenderly place among these military mementoes. The animal, a spotted saddle horse, was brought back by the General, and was occasionally rode on special military parades. The animal had become blind, and was nearly deaf, but when the band of music struck up the old war tunes and national airs, the gallant steed would prance in the field of pasture and run as if to prepare for battle. All the old fire and speed would start up in his eye and limb.

He was a great favorite with the military fraternity, who, among the numerous visitors, enjoyed the royal hospitalities of the great soldier. At the grand re-union of military organizations on the General's farm about the summer of 1880, it was planned for a sham battle. The General, mounted upon old "Spot," rode before the lines of the advancing columns, and with his aids ascended an eminence. The illustrious charger stood in the proud attitude of his former glory. It was a sight to bring tears to the eyes of many an old veteran who had seen this ubiquitous horse and his rider on "The March to the Sea."

JACOB ROSE.

Jacob Rose was born March 4th, 1770, the year the Treason House was built. His death is recorded in the Rockland County *Messenger* of the date of March 4th, 1859. His father's name was Jacob, his mother's name was Anne. They were Hollanders. Extensive tracts of land were bought by them at $2.50 and $5.00 per acre. He was a sailor. He was but ten years of age at the time of the capture of Stony Point, though the exact year of his birth is not known, which leaves the bare possibility of his having been more than ten years old when he visited the grounds the next day after the battle; but having lived all his life near the Point, and having many times served as a guide to hundreds of visitors, and on many important public occasions related the incidents of the time and place, it is perfectly safe to say that the statements given by his son Isaac are authentic. His residence with his father, Jacob, was near the locality where L. Termansen, the decorator's new cottage stands. The family of Mr. Rose distinctly heard the cannonading on the memorable night, as did also many of the neighbors. The father of Jacob Rose was, at that time, in the American army, but not in the engagement here; so that the current story that the son accompanied his father to the battle scene the next morning is not correct. He was accompanied by a number of citizens, for many of the men and women, hearing of the great American victory, ran over the next morning and on the succeeding day, to see the sight, the captured stores, examine the garrison, and witness the burial of the dead. There were many wounded men to be cared for. Friends ministered to these by furnishing delicacies to them. Water from the spring at the foot of the hill near the marsh, on the south side of the promontory, was the "balm" for the gun-shot wounds. The writer was for many days an assistant in the ambulance corps at Gettysburg, and poured many scores of canteens of pure water on the wounds of unfortunate soldiers. None but those who have witnessed similar scenes can imagine the picture of wounded and dying soldiers after a day's slaughter in battle.

Child-like, the patriot boy picked up a gun, but on going further on, saw another which he thought was finer; so, dropping the first, he selected this second one, but on still further strolling, he saw a third one, which pleased him still better, and with which he retired to his mountain home, and for fear of detection, concealed the weapon in a hollow log in the woods near his home.

At the close of the war he handled his valuable find with less fear of molestation, and when, in course of time, his father sold the weapon for $12, the boy's heart was broken. Many times $12 would doubtless not tempt Capt. Isaac Rose to give up the relic if its possession could be regained.

The testimony of the old man was that the garrison of the British extended west from the lighthouse as far as the high point next to the West Shore Railroad. Here were encamped two companies of the King's Grenadiers. These were the picked soldiers of uniformly large size, and when confronting the foe, presented a most formidable body of infantry. They were dressed in red coats with silver buttons. The buttons were as large as the knobs used on the horns of cattle to prevent their goring.

The aged man was invited at the time of the founding of the projected Wayne Monument to assist in the location of the spot which was to represent the center of the garrison. According to our map this foundation (traces of which are still visible) was on an eminence in about the center of the enemy's works, and close by, but inside the second row of abatis, the spot most likely, where the British "Standard" which Colonel Fleury struck with his hand was erected. How appropriate that the monument of Wayne, when erected, should be built on this very spot where the British Standard floated on that memorable July night.

The father of our sketch and traditional young hero was, at the time of the storming of our Fort, in another portion of the Continental Army, but had at some earlier period, most probably, come home on a furlough. It was at the time of this visit with his family, and probably having come home to assist in gathering the crops, concerning the loss of which Colonel Hays says there was great complaint, that the tragedy of his hanging was so nearly completed. Scouts from the British camp having found him, threatened his death unless he would divulge the whereabouts of a portion of the American Army that were then encamped in the vicinity of "Thiell's Mill." The noose of the rope had been fastened about his neck; only the cries and entreaties of his family caused the red-coats to desist.

CATHARINE DAVIS.

Catherine Davis, aged 85, widow of Wm. B. Davis and aunt of Mrs. James W. Fowler, says that her mother-in-law, Mary Davis, then living in Connecticut, often related to her incidents which she knew to be true concerning the war. She says the name of the colored man was Jack instead of Pompey, and that he was a slave in the family of Matthew Benson, a relative of Mr. R. B. Marks. The colored man farmed for Mr. Benson.

One day "Jack" was invited to dine with the American Generals. He said to his mistress afterwards, "If I could have had that dinner by myself I would have enjoyed it, but I did not like to dine before so many distinguished men."

One time he rode up to the house of Mrs. Benson, and sitting braced up in the saddle of his fine horse, said, in a very pompous way, "Marsa Missa, I wish I war de only man now liben about here." Said Mrs. Benson, "Then what would you do, Jack?" "Why, Missey, you see I go round on dis hoss and sell the land." "But," interrupted the lady, "who would you sell it to if you were the only citizen?" Jack had not thought of that important part of the land scheme.

Mrs. Maria Polhemus, 13 Prospect Place, N. Y. City, furnished items of interest. Her ancestors were among the first settlers, and related many incidents concerning the French and Indian War. The traditions of the Revolution which have come down through her mother's family are quite valuable. She says Jas. Lamb was her grandfather, and that the colored man was the slave of that family. He was sent each day ostensibly to sell vegetables to the British garrison, but that the real purpose was to obtain information as to the most feasable points of attack, the route, etc. It was this negro who piloted Gen. Wayne up the path that led to the enemy's works.

The women of the Revolution deserve honorable mention. The Fort next above us (Clinton) witnessed one of the most extraordinary scenes ever transacted on the Hudson. It was the case of Deborah Sampson, of Penn. On the enlistment of her husband in the army commanded by Brigadier-General Irvine, she left her home and joined her husband in camp and on the field of war.

At the assault on Fort Clinton in 1777 she seized up the port fire which her frightened husband had dropped, and fired the last cannon before the garrison was seized by the enemy.

The graphic photo-engraving from the sketch of the master-artist, Kelly, which gave Captain Molly, as she is known in history, the great and signal courage of taking the place of her husband, who fell at his post at Monmouth, has given a glory to her military life which will commemorate her deeds for all time. She handled the rammer, which was left in the cannon's mouth by her stricken husband, and cried with the voice of a true heroine, calling loudly for vengeance on the murderers of her husband.

At subsequent promotions in the great gifts of the noble-hearted Commander-in-Chief, she was breveted and commissioned by way of recognition of her unusual and great bravery.

She was a regular pensioner on the roll of Revolutionary soldiers, and, it is said, received half pay for life. She died near Highland Falls, Orange Co.

Wm. E. Garrison, born at Fort Montgomery, April 8, 1818, and a life-long resident of our town, is the authority for the following bit of tradition. He was acquainted with a man by the name of Henry Beele, who helped in making the gallant assault on the Fort. He relates that he told him that the attack was made at midnight, and that seventy-two English were killed. His grandfather, Wm. House, now dead sixty years, said the same, and also that the American forces numbered 400 and the British

600. He also stated the location of Sandy Beach as being one mile above Fort Montgomery, that being the point from which Wayne started at noon on the day preceding the attack. He has plowed the ground along this Beach many times, and claims to have found a silver button, which probably had been lost there by the English. He was also acquainted with John James, of Fort Montgomery, grandfather to Mrs. Jacob Rose, and with Billy Parr, of Highland Falls, a farmer, and uncle to Richard Cronk.

CHAPTER X.

RELICS.

ONE of the most interesting relics found in the vicinity of the battle ground is an empty bomb-shell, whose engraving forms the initial design at the head of this paragraph. It was found in the sand when the laborers were digging the foundations for the store of the Tompkins' Cove Lime Co. It is still in a fine state of preservation. For forty years or more it has lain about the store to have its record repeated and its history discussed. The weight of the missile is $42\frac{1}{2}$ pounds, its diameter being 8 inches. The thickness of the shell is $1\frac{1}{4}$ inches, and it has an opening the size of an inch auger. During all its history in the store it has contained some article which rattled on moving the ball. Assisted by Mr. W. T. Searing, we fished out the article, and found it to be a pine stopper with a hole running through it one-third of an inch in size. This was undoubtedly the fuse stopper of the bomb, which, with it, was fired from a vessel, or possibly the Point itself. A large cannon ball was also for many years in the possession of the family of Mr. Searing's father. One day, in the absence of Mr. Searing, the junior Searing sold the ball to the junk man for old iron. Curiously, the missile was covered with sole leather, probably to make it fit the cannon more perfectly. Suffice it to say, the junk man wasn't going to pay for old leather, nor was the young merchant, already showing pure business integrity, willing he should. The jack knife made a clean job of it to suit both parties.

ANOTHER relic is here presented. The wood from which it was made was taken from an immense willow which stands at the edge of the river near the old dock of King's Ferry. It stands on the very ground over which Colonel Stewart's men marched as they filed round the north side of the hill on the night of the assault. The nippers were carved by the ingenious D. Keesler, our town artist and painter, and photographed and engraved by the Photo Engraving Co., New York, who did all the engraving for this book from photographs made by Geo. O. Bedford, Haverstraw, N. Y.

Among the many visitors to these noted places was Wm. H. Seward, who cut a stick from the Washington Tree from which to make a cane. Bits of bark and twigs of the tree have gone to all portions of the country, and adorn the cabinets of many curiosity hunters.

RELICS.

BY the courtesy of Mr. Watson Tompkins, we have this cut which represents the photograph of an axe found on the site of the old Magazine of the Garrison by Roswell McElroy while in the employ of Mr. Tompkins. The letters "C A" are stamped on its side, leaving no doubt that the tool was the property of the Continental Army.

Relic hunters, before going to the battle ground, would do well to study our comprehensive map of the hill. It is one of the most interesting studies in connection with the Revolution. Though much of the ground on the north and west has since been under the cultivation of the plow, yet the rocky eminences are intact, and present the same contour as when the cannon boomed across their rugged brows.

THE mantle here shown is the veritable one around which the Smith family circle was often formed. Here, it is said, Aaron Burr read law when a young man. He was but nineteen years old at the commencement of the Revolution, and twenty-four when the scenes were enacted in the Treason House which gave it its great historic significance. The mantle is white marble and of English design, having been imported. The scrawl made by a sharp pointed instrument on the shelf of the mantle, in the tradition is said to be an attempt at writing the name "Burr." The letters "B" and "u" are quite distinct, but the following two have more the appearance of "ll," and if intended for "rr," are poor imitations of those letters. It is altogether possible the writing was done by Burr, but of the certainty no one can say.

On the memorable spot of the old Fort of Stony Point the Government erected a Lighthouse in the year 1826. The sounds of its doleful fog bell often mingle with the music of the distant church bells. This light is one of the most approved, and serves as a guide to the hundreds of vessels that pass nightly round the jutting rock of the promontory on which it stands.

It marks the spot where the British map says the "temporary Magazine" was erected.

The following relics have been found by the keepers of the Lighthouse, the family of Alax Rose, deceased, viz.: cannon ball, grape shot, bullets, chain, etc. They may be seen at the Museums of West Point and Washington's Headquarters, Newburg. It was a simple oversight that a cabinet of the relics found on the ground was not collected. Three hundred persons annualy visit these grounds. For thirty-four years the present family have been in charge of this important Government trust.

The name "Bucklebergh" is derived from the incident of coupling teams at the time when cannon were drawn over the mountain of the Highlands, which is locally known as "Bucklebergh" mountain.

Mr. A. D. Marks speaks of finding an ancient door lock in one of the closets of the Treason House. Its size was 6 x 15 inches and 2 inches thick, of solid oak, containing an iron bolt and having an iron key about 8 inches long. It was, no doubt, one of the first locks used in the old Smith House before the Revolution.

RELICS.

THE dagger initial "T" is an interesting relic. Its authenticity cannot be questioned, as it bears on the guard the stamp of the American Eagle. The arrow heads so finely engraved and added to the above letter speak of a race who consumed themselves by war. The dagger is 19 inches long, and including the handle, is 25 inches. The blade is corrugated. Its hilt is brass. The relics are the property of W. Tompkins.

The dagger was found by Mr. Lansing Hoyt under the floor of an old barn which stood neer the site where Mr. J. B. Hastings' store and residence now stand. Mr. Hoyt sold the weapon to Mr. Watson Tompkins, who kindly ordered it photographed for our use.

Enos Jersey found the "Clay dog" shown in our engraving, in the year 1881, while in the employ of G. G. Allison on the Conger Property, Grassy Point. There were two others found; the one was 4 ft. 2 inches long by $2\frac{1}{2}$ inches wide and $3\frac{1}{4}$ inches thick; the other was in the shape of a butcher's chopper. While they are of the exact material of the clay, they are at the same time of the hardness of sandstone.

Isaac Jersey, uncle to Enos Jersey, has in his possession a rifle which the great grandfather of the latter carried in the Revolution, and was also used by Enos' grandfather (Peter Jersey) in the War of 1812.

Mr. Enos Jersey also has a relic which he values. It is a short deer horn which was taken from a deer shot by Peter Jersey one hundred and eight years ago on South Mountain.

LONG years ago, while the teams of the Tompkins family were breaking up the ground on the arcable parts and north side of the hill on Stony Point, the plow turned up old terraced grounds, which revealed traces of an old encampment. The balls composing our initial letter are among the collection of W. Tompkins' cabinet.

The Revolutionary house, whose engraving we have secured from a pencil sketch drawn by Mr. Allison, the deceased son-in-law of W. Tompkins, was known as the Tobias Waldron Residence. This, with the King's Ferry House and the one whose framing timbers have entered into the house and barn of Wm. H. Rose, were known as in existence in the early days of the Revolution.

Among the cannon balls of our "L" initial is one, a nine pounder, which was also found by Mr. Hoyt. He was plowing the garden near his house, and turned up the ball from a depth of 10 inches. The ball was undoubtedly lodged there by being discharged from the English cannon on Stony Point. The cannon employed there were principally ranged in the direction of Mr. Hoyt's place, and could easily have sent a ball across the hill or "ridge" back of Mr. Hoyt's house and intervening the house and Fort. There were nine cannon stationed in the various parapets of the Garrison.

"Kossets" Cove is probably the old name known for the beach, which extends from the store of R. B. Stalter to the Point. In the locality south-west of the stable of Allison, Wood & Allison, and under the grade of the West Shore Rail Road, is a famous spring which very anciently bore the name of "Kossets Spring," from the incident of an old Indian's residence there.

Mr. L. Hoyt showed us a sword that was carried in the War

of 1812 by Captain Aaron Decamp, the grandfather of Mrs. Lansing Hoyt. It was also used by Captain John M. Decamp when he was Captain of the militia.

Margaret Springstead, aged 93, of sound mind and remarkable memory, furnished the following items of Revolutionary data. Her father was Lawrence Higgins; her mother was Margaret Scott. She is the mother of Mrs. Abram Rose.

She remembers when a girl hearing many of the old people speak of the war. Robert Allison, an aged man, was a shoemaker, and went from house to house, as was the custom of the day, to make up the shoes for the families in the community. It was while he was staying at her father's that she heard him describe the taking of Stony Point. That he was in that portion of the army that passed over at the Mud Bridge. She also learned that the troops which had come up to the "Springsteel" House had come from Fort Montgomery, and that he was with the army on that march. Allison told her that at the "Springsteel" house the men sewed white muslin and paper on their hats that they might be distinguished from the enemy in the engagement that night. This "white cockade" was ordered by General Washington in his "Orders to Wayne." She said the name of the Springsteel at whose house Wayne stopped and took supper was David, and that he was an old man before he married and that he afterwards married a young lady.

She said the place where the men rested at Springsteel's was now known as Adam's Meadow, and that Paul Rose now lived there. It was very commonly talked in her girlhood days that when the British General was captured in the Garrison, some of them were found in their beds. She also states that the conduct of the General's wife at the time of his arrest was most disgraceful, and that she was reproved for it, and that she was entreated to remain quiet, as her conduct only made matters worse; from which we infer she must have shown some grit and passion.

Mattie Benson lived in the stone house near Haverstraw.

The British had built a two-story house on the Point, and many of the citizens went over on Sundays, and that the Point was a place of resort for many years.

She lived, when first married, in the house at King's Ferry, and her daughter, now Mrs. Rose, was obliged to walk from there to Knight's Corner to school, crossing the "Mud Bridge," daily.

Iron Hill was to the south-east of the house, and it was just back of that hill that the soldiers were buried. Here were a number of graves, which for many years were kept sodded and their headstones in repair.

One day Mrs. Springsteel was planting peas in her garden, when Jacob Lent came along and said, "Right where you are planting those peas, I saw a soldier buried. He was the tallest man I have ever seen." He was, probably, one of the King's "Grenadiers."

She had the Spring dug while she lived at King's Ferry.

A Mrs. Benjamin Jones often related to her the great fear she had when there was no ferrying going on, for while armies were passing she felt safe, but ordinarily it was lonely and unsafe.

Call's Dock was built by Nicholas Call. He and his son kept a store there, for the custom, mainly, of the men who ran sloops. Hall's Dock was built farther down, for the convenience of the Lighthouse.

CHAPTER XI.

THE CELEBRATION.

FROM commanding heights could be seen the gorgeous reception given the French troops on their return from the Yorktown victory.

The procession and naval display of the Army of the Hudson, as it wound down from its encampments of New Windsor, Fishkill, West Point and other military posts, including the guards and garrisons of our own locality, and the gathering patriots who had previously bivouaced in the hills of the Highlands, presented one of the most brilliant pictures of triumphal processions known at that early day. This procession, in point of magnificence, shows the pride of Washington in everything that pertained to a well-equipped army. He was constantly teaching his men, both by precept and example, that a clean uniform and good morals were marks which commanded the highest respect.

The following order, given at Newburg, August 30, 1782, is the highest illustration ever given of the minuteness, precision and military display which characterized the Father of our Country, who says himself that he hopes "the officers will exert themselves to have the movement made with grand order and regularity." The order reads:

"Precisely at 5 o'clock to-morrow the General is to beat, on which the tents and baggage of the second Connecticut and third Massachusetts brigades are to be put in the boats. At 9 o'clock

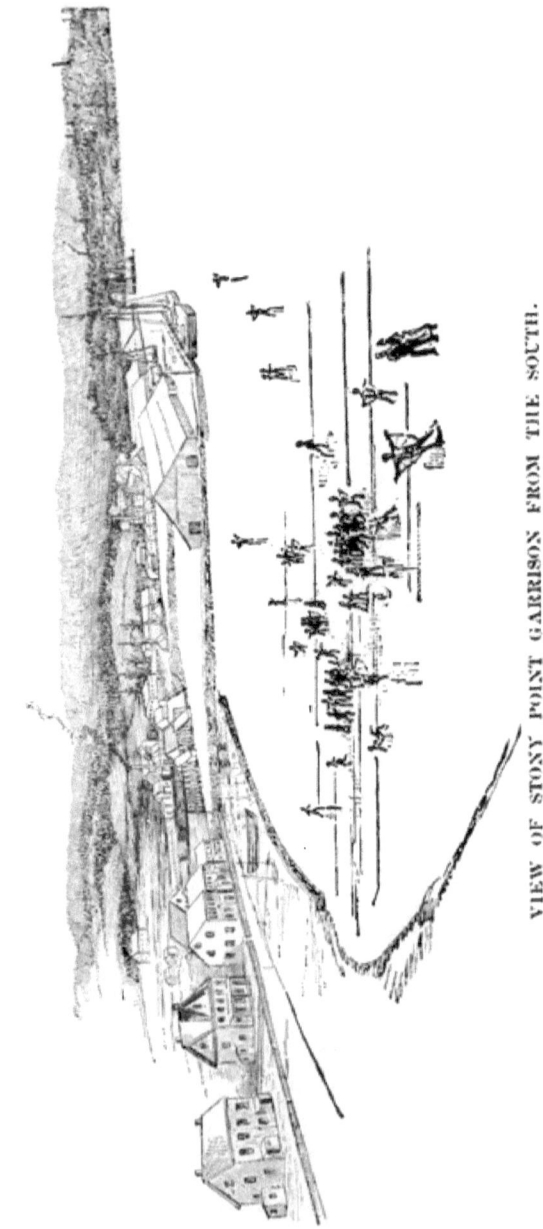

VIEW OF STONY POINT GARRISON FROM THE SOUTH.

the Assembly will beat, when these brigades are immediately to march and embark by the right, proceeding in one column to Verplanck's Point in the following order: 1st Conn., 2d Conn., 1st Mass. and 2d Mass. Brigades.

"The leading regiment of the 1st Connecticut Brigade is to advance 200 yards as a vanguard, and detach one company, which is to keep abreast and far enough apart to keep from interfering. The companies will embark as they are found on the parade, and observe that order; the Colonel to be on the right, the Lieutenant-Colonel on the left, and between each regiment there is to be a space of 75 yards; between the brigades, 150 yards; and between the divisions, 250 yards. The general officers commanding divisions and brigades are to be at the head of their respective columns, the Major-General 50 yards, and the Brigadier 25 yards in advance of them.

"As soon as the troops have embarked and taken their distances (the van opposite Little Dick's Ferry or Meigs' Redoubt) the rear brigade will beat March, which will be repeated to the front as a preparative; three cannon will be fired from the park at West Point, and the column will immediately get under motion, the music of the different regiments playing alternately if the situation of the boats will admit of it. The Inspector of Music will regulate the beat.

"If any boat should prove too leaky, break its oars, or from any other cause is unable to keep the line, it is to turn out and follow after in such manner as the prudence of the officer commanding shall see fit.

"No batteaux are to be without a commanding officer in them. The general staff of the army, except the Inspector, Adjutant and Quartermaster-Generals (who may assist in preserving order and regularity in the movement) and all the baggage which is not in boats with the troops, are to follow at a distance of half a mile in the rear, agreeably to the order that they may receive from the Quartermaster-General.

"Guards, Generals and Staff officers are not to join their corps in the movement, but they may assist in transporting the baggage by water, in order to prevent the necessity of wagons. This by no means to be drawn as a precedent in future.

"No woman to be admitted into the boats on any pretence whatever.

"If the boats are insufficient to transport the troops, with their baggage, without crowding or overloading, the surplusage will march by land under proper officers. The soldiers will take care to fill their canteens with water before they embark, as they will have no landing for water afterwards.

"The artillery annexed to brigades will proceed by land and join their respective corps at Verplanck's Point.

"SIGNALS BY DAY.

"1st. If any brigade or regiment in the rear is unable to keep up, the Brigadier commanding it is to be informed and will cause a white flag to be hoisted in the boat where he is, which will be repeated by every Brigadier (and com.) ahead, on which the leading Brigade is to move slower.

"2d. If the rear would move faster, the front will be notified by a blue flag hoisted and repeated as above.

"3d. For landing, the regimental colors will be hoisted by the landing regiment, repeated throughout the line, and kept displayed till the landing is effected, and the troops get to the ground.

"4th. If a halt should be found necessary on the passage by the Commander-in-Chief, or officer at the head of the column, it will be communicated by hoisting both flags (blue and white) on board of the boats of the Brigadiers ahead so as to be distinctly seen, and repeated as quick as possible to the rear, upon which the boats will lay by on their oars, and take great care to preserve their place and distance in line.

"SIGNALS BY NIGHT.

"1st. For moving slower, a musket will be fired and repeated by the Brigadiers, as in the day signal.

"2d. For moving faster, two guns in like manner.

"3d. For landing, three ditto.

"4th. For halting, a halt must be called, beginning in the front, and repeated from one Colonel to another distinctly, three times to the rear, to prevent mistakes and the confusion which would consequently follow.

"When the signal for landing is given, the boats are to close up without crowding, and row for the shore, and fall in by the left of each other, in which order they are to debark at their respective landing places assigned to them on the bank, and form in brigade columns as usual. In this order, the head of each column will be conducted by the Brigade Quarter-master to the right of its encampment, when it will display to the left, and each regiment repair to its own camp, stack their arms, bring up their tents and baggage, and establish themselves.

"The Quartermaster-General will furnish the commanding officers of brigades with the signal flags, which are carefully to be preserved by the Brigade Quartermasters.

"The General persuades himself that the officers will exert themselves to have the movement made with grand order and regularity."

THE GREAT CELEBRATION OF THE CESSATION OF HOSTILITIES,
APRIL 19, 1783.

The following is a copy of the orders of Washington, dated April 18, 1783, and explain themselves:

TOMPKINS COVE LIME COMPANY.

"The Commander-in-Chief orders the cessation of hostilities between the United States and the King of Great Britain to be publicly proclaimed to-morrow, at twelve, at the New Building; and that the Proclamation which will be communicated herewith be read to-morrow evening at the head of every regiment and corps of the army; after which the Chaplain with the several Brigades will render thanks to Almighty God for all His mercies, particularly for his overruling the wrath of man to His glory, and causing the rage of war to cease among the nations.

"Although the Proclamation before alluded to extends only to the prohibition of hostilities, and not to the annunciation of a general peace, yet it must afford the most rational and sincere satisfaction to every benevolent mind, as it puts a period to a long and doubtful contest, stops the effusion of human blood, and opens the prospect to a more splendid scene, and, like another Morning Star, promises the approach of a brighter day than has hitherto illuminated the Western Hemisphere. On such a happy day, which is the harbinger of peace, a day which completes the eight years of the war, it would be ingratitude not to rejoice; it would be insensibility not to participate in the general festivity.

"The Commander-in-Chief, far from endeavoring to stifle the feelings of joy in his own bosom, offers his most cordial congratulations on the occasion to all the officers of every denomination, to all the troops of the United States in general, and in particular to those gallant and persevering men who had resolved to defend the rights of their invaded country so long as the war should continue.

"For these are the men who ought to be considered as the pride and boast of the American army, and who, covered with well-earned laurels, may soon withdraw from the field of glory to the more tranquil walks of civilized life.

"Whilst the General recollects the almost infinite variety of scenes through which we have passed with a mixture of pleasure, astonishment and gratitude; while he contemplates the prospect before us with rapture, he cannot help wishing that all the brave men (of whatever condition they may be) who have shared in the toils and dangers of effecting this glorious revolution, of rescuing millions from the hand of oppression, and of laying the foundation of a great empire, might be impressed with a proper idea of the dignified part they have been called to act (under the smiles of Providence) on the stage of human affairs. For happy, thrice happy shall they be pronounced hereafter who have contributed anything, who have performed the meanest office, in erecting this stupendous fabric of freedom and empire on the broad basis of independency; who have assisted in protecting the rights of human nature, as establishing an asylum for the poor and oppressed of all nations and religions.

"The glorious task for which we first flew to arms being thus accomplished; the liberties of our country being fully acknowledged and firmly secured by the smiles of Heaven on the purity of our cause, and the honest exertions of a feeble people determined to be free, against a powerful nation disposed to oppress them; and the character of those who have persevered through every extremity of hardship, suffering and danger, being immortalized by the illustrious appellation of the Patriot Army.

"Nothing now remains but for the actors of this mighty scene to preserve a perfect unvarying consistency of character through the very last act, to close the drama with applause, and to retire from the military theater with the same approbation of angels and men which has crowned all their former virtuous actions.

"For this purpose, no disorder or licentiousness must be tolerated. Every considerate and well-disposed soldier must remember it will be absolutely necessary to wait with patience until peace shall be declared, or Congress shall be enabled to take proper measures for the security of the public stores.

"As soon as these arrangements shall be made, the General is confident there will be no delay in discharging, with every mark of distinction and honor, all the men enlisted for the war, who will then have faithfully performed their engagements with the public.

"The General has already interested himself in their behalf, and he thinks he need not repeat the assurance of his disposition to be useful to them on the present and every other proper occasion. In the meantime, he is determined that no military neglects or excesses shall go unpunished while he retains the command of the army.

"The Adjutant-General will have such working parties detailed to assist in making the preparation for a general rejoicing as the Chief-Engineer with the army shall call for; and the Quartermaster-General will also furnish such materials as he may want. The Quartermaster-General will, without delay, procure such a number of discharges to be printed as will be sufficient for all the men enlisted for the war; he will please apply to Headquarters for the form.

"An extra ration of liquor to be issued to every man to-morrow to drink perpetual peace, independence and happiness to the United States of America."

The following is a poem which its author had prepared to be read on the centennial celebration, but being taken sick he was obliged to return home before he could read it. We regret that our space would not allow of its insertion entire:

THE STORMING OF STONY POINT.
July 16th, 1779.
AN EPIC, BY J. L. DE NOAILLES.

'Twas in the sunny month—July—
    That month of all the year,
The nearest to Columbia's heart,
    To Freedom's sons most dear;
The natal-month of Liberty,
    Whose banners then unfurled,
Have waved o'er brilliant deeds of War,
    That *ring* throughout the word.

Upon a lonely, 'Sandy Beach,'
    That skirts a beetling height,
Which throws a shade on Hudson's stream,
    A gloom almost of night,
Had gathered then a trusty Band,
    One sultry afternoon,
For, ere another day should dawn,
    Must Stony Point be won.

Of stalwart frames and sturdy limbs,
    With souls to do and dare,
They onward march in single file,
    No craven spirit there;
Each face reflects a willing heart,
    Each heart as true as steel;
Each man a host in righteous cause
    As soon the foe shall feel.

While at their head a noble form
   Strides on in martial pride,
The hero, WAYNE! MAD ANTHONY WAYNE!
   With FLEURY by his side;
His brow firm-knit with stern resolve,
   Before to-morrow's sun,
Shall yon proud Fort be taken back,
   Shall Stony Point be won!

O'er crags, through streams and miry fens,
   Undaunted wend their way,
This Patriot band though Summer's sun
   Pours down its fiercest ray;
The 'Dunderberg' deters them not
   And soon is safely passed,
The foe's in sight, huzza! huzza!
   The foe's in sight, at last.

His 'men-of-war,' the evening gun
   Have fired with lordly brag,
While o'er the Fort defiant waves
   Great Britains' blood-red flag;
The sight has stirred each Patriot's blood
   The flint struck from each gun,
Shows by the deadly bayonet,
   Will Stony Point be won.

The drowsy watch reclines his head,
   His thoughts far o'er the deep,
And all is still but Hudson's wave
   Against the frowning steep;
But hark! the sentries challenge!
   The sharp, quick, 'who goes there?'

The 'Fort's our own,' (the countersign,)
    Rings on the midnight air.

The startled sentry's quickly seized,
    His musket's loud report
Alarms the slumbering garrison
    Within that fated Fort;
Loud beat the drums, to arms! to arms!
    Half-clad the Britons rush,
Roused from their dreams they wake to meet
    The bayonet's deadly thrust.

The 'forlorn hopes' their axes ply,
    The cannon loudly roar,
Awake the echoes of the dells,
    Resound from shore to shore;
The gallant WAYNE, though wounded,
    Is heard amid the din,
March on! 'at my column's head
    Let me be carried in.'

In frantic haste the Britons arm,
    And strike the random blow,
The sulph'rous smoke envelopes all,
    Enshrouds both friend and foe;
As o'er the walls the Stormers leap
    They read in each stern face,
Revenge for every murdered sire,
    For every home laid waste.

Despairing cries and muttered curse
    Burst out the right along,
As FEBIGER's men with bayonets fixed
    Come rushing madly on;

For 'Quarter,' beg the vanquished foe,
    Nor ask for it in vain,
The 'FORT'S OUR OWN!' the victors shout,
    And shout, and shout again!

Aye, FLEURY! pull that banner down,
    It has waved o'er many a fight,
And trailed through many a sea of blood
    But here it has no right;
'ST. GEORGE'S CROSS' is in the dust,
    The gallant work is done,
Up go the brilliant 'STARS AND STRIPES,'
    And Stony Point is won!

Now friend and foe, in soldier-graves,
    "In one red burial blent,"
Proud WAYNE, to his waiting Chief,
    Laconic word has sent;
"The fort's ours; with Colonel Johnson
    Six hundred prisoners be,
And all our men behaved as men,
    Determined to be free."

Speak softly; 'neath yon rising mound
    Lies many a gallant heart,
Who on this great, triumphant day,
    Did bravely act his part;
Tread lightly: every foot of earth
    Has drunk the crimson tide,
So freely shed this glorious morn
    That Freedom might abide.

When centuries have come and gone
    Since that eventful day,

And age on age forever flown
   Like them have passed away;
This statued-Bronze, a Nation's gift,
   When Empire's course is run,
Will mark this spot and tell the tale
   How Stony Point was won.

Though 'storied Urn,' triumphal Arch,
   Or yet sepulchral Fanes,
Are meet upon this hallowed ground,
   To glorify their manes;
This stern old rock! a grander Pile
   The Almighty Hand hath done,
Aye trumps their fame who fought the morn
   When Stony Point was won.

STONY POINT ILLUSTRATED.

PART II.

RESIDENCE OF MR. J. H. NEILLY.

CHAPTER I.

THE PROSPECT OF THE PLACE.

STONY POINT occupies a plateau on the west bank of the magnificent Haverstraw Bay, and is distant from New York City about thirty-five miles by rail.

The morning sun gilds no lovlier landscape or descends over no healthier clime. The Adirondacks and Green Mountains fade to tameness in comparison with some features of our picturesque scenery. The Highlands to the north and left, the angle of the Palisades on the south and right, mirror themselves on the bosom of our mighty Hudson, while the gentle undulations, mingling with the ravines and lesser highlands westward, add most romantic beauty to the whole.

The West Shore Railway, which, for equipment, management, comfort and popularity has no superior, runs through the entire length, not only of our village, but over all the sediment plain from the Clove Tunnel, five miles to the south, to the cut in Stony Point Promontory, and through it passes in beautiful meandering to the slopes of the lower Highlands.

Its long trains of elegant passenger coaches and immense continuous lines of freight cars emerging from beneath Mount "Thor's" lower Alp, move, for the first time since their departure from Weehawken, in full view of the upper "Tappan Zee;" but its station, which commands the grandest survey of the magnificent Haverstraw Bay, is the one engraved as the frontispiece of the 4th chapter of this volume.

Here the passenger, halting to visit the classic grounds of the Revolution, views with enraptured emotion the high battle ground of Mad Anthony Wayne on his left, and the expanse of Bay in which the "Vulture" of the British fleet lay while on her dastardly mission of treason, on the right. Here, in close proximity to the "Causeway" and "Swail," over which Wayne's intrepid veterans pushed on to the storming of the Fort, as by a special monumental designing, the West Shore's beautiful station is erected out of the bricks made from the very clay which was consecrated by the blood of the patriots who fell on that memorable night. Exhumed war missiles, such as ball and grape shot, are preserved in the cabinets of some of our families. Many have been removed to military museums, while down sunken in the marsh at the base of the side of the bold promontory are still remnants of the outer line of "Abatis." Every inch of these grounds is sacred in the annals of history, and a thousand years hence will be visited equally and as eagerly as are the Pantheon of Rome or the Temples of Concord and Jupiter of Agrigentum of Greece.

Standing on these grounds the transient habitue, as well as the permanent dweller, feels that he is on sacred soil. None visit our quiet hamlet but to laud its physical beauties and resort to its classic scenes; while the natural scenery is a subject of like interest to foreign and native artists.

Here the moral tone is elevated, and the sanctuary privileges are equal to those of any rural village.

The natural advantages are proverbial. The great Metropolis of the Continent would be seriously retarded in her material progress without us. Manhattan would be bleaker and less substantial without

"Our tempered clay in moulded brick complete."

RESIDENCES OF GEO. S. ALLISON, W. H. WILES AND CHARLES A. WILES.

Hundreds of millions of bricks are annually sent from our shores.

It is truly enchanting to sit on a cottage balcony on a Summer evening and see the great steamers, like brilliant floating castles, move up and down the river. In the silvery light of the moon, or under the star-lit sky, how different from the

> " Low sound of leaves and splash of oars,
> And lapsing waves on quiet shores,"

of some inland wood-bound lake.

CHAPTER II.

FISHING.

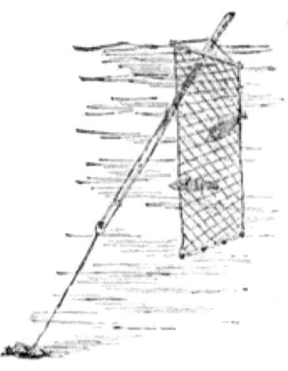

THE fishing of the Bay, once a business yielding a fair income to those who followed it, has of late become less profitable. Among the early fishermen were John Leet, David Lawrence, John Bulson, John Ten Eyck, Hiram Phillips, Patrick and Thomas Reilly, Eugene Piero and Caleb Gilleo, who did more or less fishing.

A good record is also made by Harris and Jacob Lent. Those engaged particularly in shad fishing were Wm. Weiant, Geo. B. Fowler, and their assistants.

Wm. I. Owen has tried various devices, and has disturbed the happiness of many fishes of many kinds.

Shad are caught in large quantities in the Spring from April to June. Once or twice in a season a sturgeon gets entangled in the drift net. They have been caught measuring 9 feet in length, weighing 200 to 400 lbs. Seines are from 600 to 900 feet long. The set line or "trawl" is used for catching striped bass and eels. The drift net is a popular device. The length of it is sometimes 2000 feet, and has a depth of 25 feet. The net is kept in an upright position by a row of buoys of wooden blocks fastened to the top line 18 ft. apart. Iron rings, from 6 in. to 8 in. in diameter, are fastened to the bottom or ground line to correspond with the floating blocks. The meshes of this kind of net are $4\frac{3}{4}$ to 5 inches. The nets are allowed to float with the tide for several hours, during which time the shad, in attempting to pass up the river, find themselves fast by the gills in the meshes of the net. In olden times the gill net was fastened to poles set in the mud of the river. Some have been driven as deep as 14 ft. Poles 60 ft. in length were sometimes used. The timber being green would naturally sink. When conveyed by boat to the spot where they were to be driven, the buts, which had been previously sharpened, were allowed to sink while the tops were held on to. By fastening a cross-beam to this top, the weight of a number of men would force the stick down into the mud of the river bottom. These poles were usually set 20 ft. apart. Our cut shows one of the most unique nets for catching bass and perch. This style is called T net. We accompany the engraving with the following description, viz.: A stick of hemlock, chestnut or other light lumber, about 16 ft. long, is anchored at one end by a cable and stone; the other end is allowed to stick up in the water. Within a few feet of the top are bored two holes to receive hickory withes, which suspend the floating stick, to which the net is attached as seen in the picture. The net is usually about 15 ft. square, and, being well weighted, it stands in an upright position, the entire fixture being held in position in low water by the heavy sinkers at the end of the long hemlock timber. As the tide moves up or down, the net can freely adapt its position to its movement. The fish are caught in the meshes as they are in drifts. Sometimes 15 or 20 of those T nets are set across the river by one fisherman. This same style of net is also used in fishing on ice. Long openings are cut in the ice, and the nets let down through these apertures.

Common fikes are set with wings 8 to 10 feet long. Eel pots, made up of splints about 4 feet long, and baited with "menhaden," or herring, or scraps of fish, etc., are useful devices to catch certain kinds of fishes. As high as 30 lbs. have been caught in a single fike.

The angler still goes fishing for sport. In the season of shad fishing persons from the country come long distances to purchase a supply of shad. Newburgh and New York City are the principle markets.

CHATER III.

THE GEOLOGY OF STONY POINT.

BY PROF. J. F. KEMP.

THE triangular area of Stony Point Township includes a series of different kinds of rocks, whose diversity is quite surprising when the attention is closely directed to them. Their general relations are as follows: The great ridge of the Palisades ceases where the Haverstraw tunnel of the West Shore Railway breaks through. The hard, compact rock of which it is formed gives place to red sandstones, shales and conglomerates, which stretch away to the north, underlying Haverstraw and the southern portion of Stony Point. On the river bank they are covered up by the clay beds, but inland they reveal their presence by the red color of the soil, which results from their disintegration.

They reach north well into Stony Point, forming the cliffs along the brook below the main street of the village.

Their northern limit runs from a point southwest of the old M. E. Church, diagonally northeast to the small cut on the West Shore Railway between Stony Point Station and the Point itself.

Near the above-named church the red sandstone is succeeded by a tough, dark-gray rock, and this again by the light-gray gneiss on which the church itself is built. Along the highway from Stony Point to Tompkin's Cove, the red sandstone is succeeded by the blue limestone, which is probably a continuation of the dark gray rock above referred to. But, on the West Shore track, we meet first a contorted mica schist, whose twisted layers afford some surfaces in the cut like the grain of curly maple, and, second, the heavy black rock of which the greater part of the Point is formed.

Strange to say, on the top of the promontory are some stray pieces of limestone entirely surrounded by this black rock, exactly as if it had picked them up when flowing in a melted condition like lava. Following the railroad track, a lighter colored brown granite succeeds, and then, after crossing the Cove, a few feet of slaty rock, and then the quarries in the blue limestone. Along the highway the red sandstone is succeeded, as has been already stated, by the blue limestone. The limestone gives place, just north of Connor's Hotel, to the gneiss, which stretches unbroken to the Highlands.

Further inland, however, we meet, just north of the St. George's M. E. Church, along the roadside near the old parsonage, a dark, black rock similar to Stony Point, which runs along the gneiss in an irregular line north east to Henry Keesler's, appearing also in small amount to the east of his house. At the blacksmith shop of Warren Brooks on Duck Cedar Brook a good exposure is seen. But a short distance north the gneiss again reappears, and stretches away to the Highlands. West of the brook at the lime kiln is a bed of fine white and veined marble, which might furnish a beautiful ornamental stone if properly prepared. The hills, however, are gneiss.

RILEY & ROSE'S BRICK YARD.

This brief description details the rocks fairly well, and it simply remains to say a word about their relations to the neighboring region.

The red sandstone does not cross the Hudson. The country there is chiefly formed of the gneiss and the black rocks of Stony Point and the blue limestone.

Back of Verplanck's Point, along the contact between the black rock and the gneiss, some emery has been mined, and also inland near Colebaugh Pond.

Similar emery may be found in Stony Point north of the St. George's M. E. Church, but it is to be said that the mines across the river are no longer worked, and were never much of a success.

The clay beds of Grassy Point and the beach are, however, of great value, and will furnish employment and livelihood for many people for many years to come.

They are sediments which have been deposited by the Hudson River on the rocks already mentioned, when the river was larger than now, and set back on its banks as far as the clay beds are found. If any leaves or shells should be found in the clay beds they should be preserved, as they are of great interest to those familiar with them.

The Tompkin's Cove limestone is a valuable stone, and useful for a great variety of purposes.

The other rocks, however, are of no practical value, and are interesting only from their diversity.

There is no probability of anything being found in them valuable enough to pay for digging it out.

The "clay dogs" found in the clay bed are curious. There were found by Enos Jersey some fine specimens.

STORE OF CHARLES MARKS & BROTHER.

CHAPTER IV

MUSIC.

THE morals and refining arts have received due attention. Yet it was not always so. The early muses of poetry and and music did not seem, at the first, to find this fairy land, but passed right on through the lower gates of the Highlands in search of broader, but, alas! less fruitful fields, to ply their shrilling pibrochs among the Highlanders of the Hudson. They searched only for the hire of the chivalrous knights of Revolutionary fame, while here in "Mohammed's Paradise," or this veritable Pantheon of the gods, lived true earls of moral luxury and noted barons of undoubted wealth. Had the provincial settlers counselled with the sages of the ennobling art of lyric music, a softer pathos and more refining imagery would have filled the minds of our otherwise intelligent populace.

Happy, however, for the present generation that the incipient love of the sacred science of vocal music, and the elevating and evangelizing art of instrumental harmony, have been recently introduced, and that noteworthy contributions of promising talent are being made to this very commendable passion and accomplishment. Show me the community devoid of love for music, and you have pointed to a sure evidence of degrading superstition. Music is an antidote to all forms of it. Hazlitt never said a truer saying, respecting the mission of music, than the following: "The sound which the stream of high thoughts carried down the future

VIEWS ON HUDSON STREET.

ages makes as it flows—deep, distant murmuring evermore, like the waters of the mighty ocean." Thoughts that would perish like diamonds dropped into the sea, are borne aloft and conveyed to the chambers of the higher intellect by the fragrant air of music. How many precious interpretations of Eternal Truth are unconsciously imbibed in song and melody! It was born in Heaven. The morning stars sang together at Creation's dawn. Harps of gold are used in Paradise. David, the ancient sweet singer of Israel, may now be teaching the infant millions the song of righteousness, and Miriam leading the choir of the one hundred and forty-four thousand in the rendering of the poem commemorative of Israel's escape at the Arabian Gulf. Only her leadership, perchance, could guide the sonata of that immortal song of Moses, before whom the ancient Celtic bards, Sappho and Horace, with lyre and guitar, may mingle with the harpers of the Great King led in their celestial music by her once rude timbrel but now heavenly instrument. How vividly the memory of those sounds must revive the images of the past. All ages and peoples, of any hue and condition, had their music.

CHAPTER V.

THE CHURCHES.

THE TOMPKIN'S COVE M. P. CHURCH.

THE Tompkin's Cove M. P. Church (see page 29) was organized June 3rd, 1843, Rev. E. W. Griswold, pastor. Of those who were then members only four survive, and only one (Sally Odell) is still a member, the other three having moved away.

For the first six years following the organization, there is no detailed account that has been preserved of the deaths and removals, etc. Since that time, including the original members organized, 412 persons have been received into full membership. Of these 46 have died members of the church in hope, 175 have moved away with letters of dismissal, 63 have dropped from the rolls as backsliden, 3 have withdrawn by request of the pastor, 1 has been expelled, 112 are still members of the church. This leaves 10 unaccounted for in consequence of the imperfection of the record for the first six years.

The Society is in a good condition, financially and otherwise. When taken altogether, perhaps, it was never stronger than it is to-day.

CHURCH OF THE IMMACULATE CONCEPTION.

This building was erected in the year 1861 during the pastorate of the late Rev. Patrick Mahoney, of Haverstraw. It is a brick structure, situated at Tompkin's Cove, about five miles from the village of Haverstraw.

Before its erection in 1861 the Catholics of this place were accustomed to hold their religious services in the old store of the Tompkin's Cove Lime Company, in which the family of an Irishman named John McGrath then resided. Here Mass was celebrated about once a month by a priest well-known to the citizens of Haverstraw as Father McKeown. This was about the year 1847. This zealous priest remained about two or three years in Haverstraw, and was succeeded by Rev. J. Scullen, who also ministered to the wants of the Catholic portion of his flock in Stony Point, and conducted the religious services on Sundays in the house of John Caffray, one of the few Catholics now surviving who were obliged at one time to walk from here to New York if

THE CHURCHES.

they desired to receive the consolations of their religion from a Catholic priest.

Rev. Patrick Mahoney succeeded Father Scullen as pastor of Haverstraw, and he, seeing the need of a commodious and suitable place of worship for the increasing Catholic population of Stony Point, commenced the erection of a church. The building was commenced on the 13th day of April, and the first Mass was celebrated on the 15th day of August, 1864.

During the pastoral charge of Father Mahoney, a day school

for children was started in the basement of the church, but, owing to the limited means of, and the gradual decrease in, the Catholic population of this vicinity, the school was not of very long duration.

In the year 1876 the Rev. Henry P. Baxter was appointed pastor at Haverstraw, and whilst under his guidance the Catholic people of this vicinity attended religious services in their church every second Sunday until the year 1886, when they resolved upon possessing a resident priest. Encouraged by their pastor to raise funds for the purpose of erecting a pastoral residence, the Catholics of this place, though few in numbers, set to work with a will. Thinking that their efforts would be more successful if they had a priest to direct them in their noble undertaking, they petitioned for a priest, and the assistant priest of Haverstraw, Rev. J. P. Brennan, was appointed as their first resident pastor. The present flourishing condition of the parish, which numbers only 75 families, bears ample testimony to the generosity and religious zeal of the Catholics in the upper portion of Stony Point.

THE PRESBYTERIAN CHURCH, STONY POINT.

In connection with the Presbyterian Church of Haverstraw, a congregation of people alike in religious views grew up within the present limits of our town. Sunday school was first established in 1845, meeting in the house of worship which had been built the previous year. From this a strong and flourishing church was soon developed. The Haverstraw Church relinquished all claims to their legal title, and the people became a separate charge.

The church was rebuilt in 1869, and now stands a commodious house of worship, as seen in our cut.

The following pastors have officiated since its organization: The Revs. Abijah Green, David Egan, Frederick King, J. J. Mc-

THE CHURCHES.

PRESBYTERIAN CHURCH.

Mahon, R. B. Mattice, T. C. Straus, and the present pastor, Rev. Mr. Gilmore.

Rev. J. S. Gilmore is the son of William and grandson of William Gilmore. Mr. Gilmore is a native of West Virginia, and was born Sept. 2, 1830. His father was born near Carlisle, Pa., in 1773. The grandfather was a native of Ireland. Mr. Gilmore's mother was Agnes Scott, the place and date of her birth being Washington Co., Pa., February 14, 1797. She was the daughter of Mary Hamilton, who was born in Westmoreland Co., Pa., in 1772. The brothers of Mr. Gilmore are William, Robert and Joseph; the sisters, Mary, Sarah Ann, and Margaret.

His wife's name before marriage, April 27, 1859, was Catharine, the daughter of George Sloane. The daughters are Mary S., Sarah A., Martha L. and Florence H.

Rev. Mr. Gilmore was called to the pastorate of the Presbyterian Church of this place October, 1884, having served formerly the following churches: The First Church of Indiana; Sullivan, Indiana; Keinett Square, Pa.; Titusville, N. J. In mission work, New York city, Fredonia Plains, N. Y., and Stony Point, N. Y., making an average of four years in seven charges. His graduations were from Jefferson College and Princeton Seminary.

THE HOUSE OF THE GOOD SHEPHERD.

In the year 1866 there was established, under the care and direction of the Rev. Ebenezer Gay, Jr., an Episcopal institution known as the House of the Good Shepherd.

Mr. Gay first came to Haverstraw in 1859 and again in 1862, when he entered upon his duties as rector of Trinity Parish. He had spent his early years in teaching in various schools, and by laborious work had succeeded in obtaining an extended education. His experience had fitted him well for the lifework before him. While ministering in his parish at Haverstraw he formed plans which matured in the establishment of a home for the orphans in the parish.

Later on, this was developed into a mission house, home and training school. At first located at Haverstraw, then moved to Garnerville, it is now located in a beautiful and commanding view upon the Hudson, a short distance above Tompkin's Cove.

The buildings consist of the home, school-house and church, all constructed under the supervision of Mr. Gay, and still under his charge.

ST. GEORGE'S METHODIST CHURCH

is situated about one mile west of the West Shore Rail Road Station at Stony Point. Its origin is dated to 1807, when Daniel Phillips opened his house for a class and became its first class leader. Among the early Methodists were Mr. Wandell, John Thiell and Rev. James Sherwood. The regular itinerants who, under God, assisted in planting early Methodism in this region, were Rev. Peter Vannest, Daniel Fidler, John Finley, Phineas

ST. GEORGE'S M. E. CHURCH.

Rice, Joseph Lybrand, Charles Pitman, George Benghart, Lawrence McCombs, Manning Force, Wm. Hibbard, Anthony Atwood, David W. Bartine. The subsequent pastors were Revs. L. M. Prettyman, Wm. Hanly, I. N. Felch, Benj. Reed, Matthew Mattison, Alex. Gilmore, Josiah F. Canfield, Mulford Day, L. R. Dunn, Joseph Ashbrook, Geo. F. Brown, Wm. M. Burrows, Fletcher Lummis, Garret Van Horn, S. D. Longheed, M. C. Stokes, W. G. Wiggins, Walter Chamberlain, F. S. Wolf, Rodney Winans, Gilbert H. Winans, J. W. Seran, David Walters, J. W. Barrett, Richard Johns, Isaac W. Cole, A. S. Campton, H. J. Hayter, J. P. Fort and E. V. King.

The present edifice was rebuilt in 1882, under the pastorate of Rev. E. V. King. It is at present connected with the charge of Thiells, Rev. C. Clark, pastor.

THE STONY POINT METHODIST EPISCOPAL CHURCH

was organized according to the law governing religious societies, Jan. 13, 1885, and assumed the above-named title because the church building or tabernacle was built in the village of Stony Point. There was no church of the name in the place. The corporate name of the old church from which the new came out had been and still is known in law as "St. George's M. E. Church of North Haverstraw."

Ecclesiastically, the new society was not recognized until the following Spring, when the annual Conference set it apart as a separate charge, giving its pastor the oversight at the same time of Garnerville. Previous, however, to the organization of this church, a few ladies, whose residences were in this part of the charge, met at the house of the late W. J. Weiant, on the evening of Oct. 9, 1884, and organized a Ladies' Aid Society. Mr. Weiant presided by request of the meeting. The first prayer meeting

STONY POINT M. E. PARSONAGE AND PROSPECTIVE CHURCH.

held in the place by this society was held in the Tabernacle, Dec. 30. There were sixteen persons present. The Sunday School was organized in the Tabernacle, Jan. 11, 1885, with 38 scholars, 5 officers and 9 teachers. The first meeting of the new Board of Trustees took place Jan. 17, 1885. There were 9 trustees, and all present.

The temporary structure in which the society worship was erected July 4, 1884, but was not enclosed until November. The cost of the building entire was about $800, and the lot was $1000. The society was duly incorporated on the day of its organization.

Its present pastor, the Author, is closing a pastorate of three years, having spent a year on the old charge, which would make four years in the same community.

The membership at the opening of the new church was 79. The number of names on the Record since has been 175, beside the probationers. The aggregate amount of money raised for all purposes during the writer's pastorate is $10,800.

Before leaving the church, we have, at no expense to them, left an engraving of a prospective edifice with the hope that in the near future the society may be able to erect something similar to it. The one shown in the cut can be built for about $5,000, and would accommodate, when properly seated, 500 persons.

CHAPTER VI.

REGISTRATION.

HE following is a list of names of the voters of Stony Point Township:

Askew, George	Stony Point	Babcock, Moses	Stony Point
Ambrey, Arthur	"	Babcock, Alfred	"
Ambrey, Willis	"	Bobb, Louis, Jr.	"
Abrams, Edward	"	Bowman, Eugene	Grassy Point
Abrams, George	"	Babcock, Augustus	Stony Point
Able, Daniel	"	Babcock, Isaac	"
Aiken, Henry	"	Brooks, O. B.	"
Ayers, Thomas	"	Basley, John W.	"
Allison, Wilbur	"	Babcock, Josiah	"
Allison, Frank	Grassy Point	Bulson, Sylvester	"
Allison, Brewster J.	Stony Point	Burris, Abram	"
Ambrey, William	"	Brennan, Michael	"
Anderson, James	Tompkin's Cove	Burris, Thomas	"
Allison, Charles	Grassy Point	Brooks, Thomas	"
Allison, John W.	"	Brooks, William	"
Applegate, Benj.	Tompkin's Cove	Belden, Wm. R.	"
Burd, Chas. W.	Stony Point	Brooks, M. V. B.	"
Basley, Wm.	"	Bulson, Jonas	Tompkin's Cove
Bulson, Duane	"	Bower, David	Stony Point
Bobb, John	Tompkin's Cove	Barns, Joseph	"
Basley, Robert	Stony Point	Blauvelt, William	"
Basley, Henry	"	Barton, Warren	"
Basley, Aaron	"	Blauvelt, Thomas	"
Basley, Thomas	"	Blauvelt, Samuel	"
Basley, Garrett	"	Blair, John	"
Brooks, John	"	Blair, William	"
Bulson, Jackson	"	Barton, James	"
Burd, Wm. H.	Tompkin's Cove	Barton, Hanford	"
Burris, Thomas	Stony Point	Burd, Charles	"
Bulson, Levi	"	Burd, Hudson	Jones' Point
Bulson, James	"	Barton, James R.	Grassy Point
Barton, Daniel	Stony Point	Ballard, Sylvester R.	Stony Point
Brush, William	"	Bulson, Alexander	"
Bulson, Richard	Grassy Point	Bower, Louis	"

Brownell, Jacob E......Stony Point	Conklin, Edmund......Stony Point
Brightmyre, Jacob...... "	Conklin, Leonard...... "
Bower, George.......... "	Conklin, Joseph........ "
Bower, Stephen H...... "	Caton, Elsworth.... "
Bulson, John A........ "	Call, Wm. J.......... "
Bulson, Hiram.......... "	Champan, Theodore.... "
Burris, Wm. H........ "	Casseles, King W...... "
Beebe, Richard........ "	Casseles, John.... "
Bulson, Wm. J........ "	Casseles, Joseph...... "
Bulson, Henry........ "	Casseles, Alonzo P...... "
Bulson, John....Fort Montgomery	Casseles, Joseph, Jr...... "
Byard, Andrew........Stony Point	Coe, Henry.........Grassy Point
Byard, Henry........ "	Coe, Gabriel........ "
Babcock, Thomas........ ....Thiells	Call, Jacob.........Tompkin's Cove
Brophy, Patrick........Grassy Point	Clancy, Felix....... "
Benson, Michael........	Connell, John...... "
Brooks, Warren........Stony Point	Connor, John....... "
Bobb, Louis, Sr..... "	Caffery, John...... "
Brooks, Brewster........ "	Crawley, Richard......Grassy Point
Bonner, Thomas ...Tompkin's Cove	Crum, George.........Stony Point
Burke, Thomas.......Grassy Point	Crum, Earnest........ "
Boldt, Christian........Stony Point	Clark, John........ "
Boldt, John .... "	Clark, Matthew....Tompkin's Cove
Ballard, Alvin S ...... "	Coleman, H. M........Stony Point
Ballard, Andrew........ "	Crum, Chester........ "
Ballard, Nelson.......... "	Duffney, Miles........ "
Brennan, Rev. Fr....Tompkin's Cove	Decker, Austin........ "
Burris, Sherman........ .....Stony Point	Dutcher, Brickenridge ...Jones' Point
Burris, Ellsworth....... "	Delanoy, Calvin........Stony Point
Corwin, Josiah.......... "	Dykins, Alonzo........ "
Clark, William........ "	Deronde, Theodore..,Tompkin's Cove
Clark, Peter.......... "	Doyle, Thomas.......Grassy Point
Coe, George........... "	Degroat, John........ "
Clancy, Frank.......... "	Deronde, William......Stony Point
Costello, James........ "	Decker, William, Jr..... "
Clark, James........ "	Davis, Henry.........Grassy Point
Clark, Frank.......... "	Delaney, Jerry, Jr...... "
Caffery, Peter...... "	Dockerty, John........ "
Cole, Jacob........... "	Dreddin, John........ "
Coe, Isaac........ "	Delaney, Jeremiah, Sr... "
Call, Everet........ "	De Groat, Chas........ "
Call, Jacob........... "	De Camp, John, Jr......Stony Point
Call, Wallace..... "	Drout, George, Jr.......Jones' Point
Courtney, John.......... "	Drout, Henry........ "
Connell, Patrick....... "	Dunn, Michael......Tompkin's Cove
Casseles, Albert....... "	Dennison, Alexander....Stony Point
Casseles, Chas. H....... "	Degau, John.......Tompkin's Cove
Casseles, James.... "	Dunn, Martin....... "
Casseles, Jeremiah..... "	Dunn, John.........Stony Point
Cavel, William B........ "	Dunn, William. ....Tompkin's Covt
Crum, Spencer.......... "	Duffney, Wm. H.......Stony Poine
Crum, Henry.......... "	De Camp, Aaron........ "

REGISTRATION.

Decker, Abram G.	Stony Point	Garrison, Prince	Stony Point
De Camp, John M.	"	Gallagher, William	Tompkin's Cove
De Camp, Matthew	"	Goetschius, Samuel	Stony Point
Decker, Wm.	"	Goetschius, Henry D.	"
Dykins, Abram	"	Goetschius, Joseph	"
Deronde, Jacob	Tompkin's Cove	Goetschius, James H.	"
De Groat, James A.	Jones' Point	Garrison, N. A., Dr.	"
Duel, Prof.	Tompkin's Cove	Grady, James	Tompkin's Cove
Dinan, Thomas	Grassy Point	Grady, Martin	"
Dykens, Alonzo	Stony Point	Hoeck, John	Stony Point
Dykens, Charles	"	Herbert, Samuel	Jones' Point
Easton, John	"	Herbert, Joseph	"
Engle, Jacob	"	Holt, Thomas	Stony Point
Engle, Peter	"	Hurd, Wm. J.	"
Forrest, Jackson	"	Hoyt, Charles	"
Finnigan, Phillip	"	Hill, Calvin T.	Tompkin's Cove
Finnigan, Irving	"	Herbert, Nathaniel	Jones' Point
Fagan, Terrance	Grassy Point	Hulse, James	Stony Point
Fox, Hugh	"	Hurd, Jackson	"
Finn, James	"	Higgins, William	Tompkin's Cove
Flyn, Michael	"	Hurd, Hudson	Stony Point
Fay, Patrick	"	Hannigan, Patrick	"
Farland, Mike	"	Hogan, James	"
Fowler, William	Stony Point	Hurd, Mathew	"
Frank, Herman	"	Hill, Silas	"
Frank, Julius	"	Halt, Albert	"
Fowler, Gilbert	Grassy Point	Hoyt, Dennis M.	"
Fowler, John	Stony Point	Hoyt, George	"
Fowler, James W.	"	Hoyt, James B.	Tompkin's Cove
Finn, Edward	"	Halt, William F.	Stony Point
Frank, Jacob	"	Hailey, Ferdinand	Tompkin's Cove
Fales, George	"	Hailey, David G.	"
Fonda, Bayard	"	Herbert, Hiram	Jones' Point
Fonda, Howard	"	Herbert, Isaac	"
Fonda, Clinton	"	Hurd, Abram	Stony Point
Gannon, S. B.	Jones' Point	Holly, Hiram	Tompkin's Cove
Goetschius, Roswell	Stony Point	Hoyt, William H.	Stony Point
Golden, John	"	Hastings, Jacob B.	"
Garrison, William	Tompkin's Cove	Hammond, Wm. K.	"
Gay, Rev. Ebenezer	"	Hilton, Henry	"
Gee, Charles	Stony Point	Harrison, C. S.	"
Gallagher, Charles J.	Grassy Point	Hazard, Daniel	"
Goldrick, Phillip	"	Hazard, James	"
Gallagher, Thomas	"	Hazard, Frank F.	"
Gallagher, B. J.	"	Hurd, David J.	"
Gallagher, Daniel	Stony Point	Hill, Henry	"
Gilleo, Caleb	"	June, Caleb	Jones' Point
Gilleo, Eugene	"	June, Lemuel	"
Gilmor, Rev. J. S.	"	Jones, James	Stony Point
Goetschius, Nelson	"	Jones, William	"
Goetschius, Eugene	"	Johnson, Harrison	"
Gallagher, Patrick	Tompkin's Cove	Jones, John J.	"

June, Andrew..........Jones' Point
Johnson, George.......Stony Point
June, Peter..............   "
Jones, William F......   "
June, David............   "
Jones, Edward..   "
James, Ambrose.....Tompkin's Cove
June, Abraham......   "
Johnson, Arthur........Stony Point
June, Baxter...........Jones' Point
Jones, John R.......... Stony Point
Jones, Charles............   "
James, Paul............   "
James, William H...Tompkin's Cove
Johnson, W. N..........Stony Point
Jersey, Enos...........Grassy Point
Kemp, Charles..........Jones' Point
Kemp, Theodore...   "
Keiser, John........Tompkin's Cove
Keiser, John, Jr.....   "
Keenan, Patrick........Stony Point
Keesler, Alexander..Tompkin's Cove
Keenen, John.......   "
Kearny, Michael...   "
Kelly, Michael... ...   "
Kelly, Michael.......   "
Keenan, James... ..   "
Kearny, James......   "
Knapp, Jacob P.........Stony Point
Keesler, Henry......   "
Knapp, Hiram G........   "
King, John............   "
Keesler, Edward........   "
Keenan, Arthur.........   "
Keesler, Bradley....Tompkin's Cove
Keenan, Edward......   "
Keenan, John.......   "
Keenan, Thos.......   "
Krusie, William.........Stony Point
Krusie, Hiram..........   "
Krusie, Charles....Tompkin's Cove
Knapp, David J........Stony Point
Knight, William.......   "
Keesler, James...... ..   "
Keesler, Daniel.........   "
Keesler, Henry......Tompkin's Cove
Keesler, Theodore...   "
King, William E. ...   "
Knapp, John............Stony Point
Knowlton, James........   "
Kochler, Chas. H......Jones' Point
Lewis, Oliver.... .....Grassy Point

Lent, Moses.........Tompkin's Cove
Lent, George........   "
Lent, Abraham......   "
Lemon, J. N..........Jones' Point
Linkletter, James........Stony Point
Linkletter, John J.......Jersey City
Lanegen, Patrick.......Grassy Point
Long, Patrick..... ..   "
Long, William..........   "
Lynch, William.....Tompkin's Cove
Lent, William H....   "
Lent, Leonard.......   "
Lent, Harris.........   "
Lent, Jacob.. .....   "
Leonard, Patrick........Stony Point
Lent, Augustus......Tompkin's Cove
Lynch, James...........Stony Point
Leach, Elijah........   "
Lilburn, Adam.............Haverstraw
Lawrence, David.......Stony Point
Leet, James......... ..   "
Lent, Alfred J..........Jones' Point
Lent, Richard..... Tompkin's Cove
Lent, William......   "
Lent, Joshua........   "
Lynch, William.........Stony Point
Leach, John T..........   "
Lynch, Daniel..........   "
Leach, Charles.........   "
Leach, George.........   "
McElroy, Roswell.......   "
McCauley, Lewis........   "
Morgan, George..... ..   "
Meehan, Martin.....Tompkin's Cove
Muray, Thos............Stony Point
Mackey, James H.......   "
Mulhail, John..........   "
Mahon, John......... ..   "
Miller, Joseph..........   "
Martin, Harson......Tompkin's Cove
Mackey, Edward........Stony Point
Miller, William........   "
Marsh, Nelson......   "
Morrisey, Patrick.......Grassy Point
Mackey, Aaron..........   "
Mulhall, Garrett........Stony Point
May, Jacob............Grassy Point
Mossieur, Paul...... ..   "
Mackey, William ......Stony Point
Munderville, John......Grassy Point
Merritt, Jeremiah.......   "
Miller, Archibald.......   "

Mulvale, Martin	Stony Point	Phillips, Hiram	Stony Point
Marsh, Stephen	"	Phillips, Nelson	"
Marsh, Alexander	"	Phillips, William	"
Mackey, Isaac	Tompkin's Cove	Payne, A. T., Attorney	"
Mead, Joseph	Stony Point	Penny, Joseph	"
McBride, Walter	"	Phillips, Daniel	"
Miller, John	"	Phillips, Edward J.	"
McMahon, Rev. J. J.	"	Peterson, Samuel	"
Marks, Abram D	"	Pymm, Stephen	"
Marks, Richard B	"	Pymm, Melville	"
Marks, Charles	"	Peterson, Charles	Tompkin's Cove
Marks, George H.	"	Peterson, Rock	Grassy Point
Mackey, David	Haverstraw	Palmer, James	Thiells
Mackey, Everet	Stony Point	Paul, Harry	Stony Point
McCauley, William	"	Paul, Samuel	"
Meehan, Patrick	Tompkin's Cove	Phillips, Nelson, Jr.	"
Martin, Charles	Stony Point	Phillips, Nelson R.	"
Meusell, Antone	"	Quelch, William	"
Nally, James	"	Rose, David W.	"
Nolan, James	"	Rose, Daniel	"
Neilley, John H	"	Reed, Alexander	"
Odell, Miles	"	Rose, Alfred	"
Odell, Lascelle	Tompkin's Cove	Rhodes, George W.	Jones' Point
Odell, Sidney	Thiells	Rose, John	Stony Point
Ogier, Wm. C.	Stony Point	Rose, George A.	"
Odell, Nelson	Thiells	Rose, Leonard	"
Olive, James	Stony Point	Rider, Oliver	Tompkin's Cove
O'Malley, Thos.	Grassy Point	Rose, Oscar	Stony Point
O'Keef, Cornelius	"	Rose, James, Jr.	"
Odell, James	Stony Point	Ryan, Thomas	Grassy Point
Odell, William	"	Rose, William	Stony Point
Odell, Henry	"	Rose, Charles B.	"
O'Brien, Michael	Tompkin's Cove	Rose, Benjamin	"
Ossman, Louis	Stony Point	Rose, Charles	"
Ossman, John	"	Rose, George	"
Oakley, Charles B	Jones' Point	Rose, Alfred	Tompkin's Cove
O Keef, John	Grassy Point	Rose, Isaac	Stony Point
O'Brian, Martin	Stony Point	Riley, Thomas	"
Odell, Charles	Thiells	Rose, Abram H.	"
Odell, Jacob	"	Rose, Daniel	"
Odell, Rutledge	Tompkin's Cove	Rose, Augustus	"
Ossman, Joseph	Grassy Point	Rose, Benton	"
Osborn, Daniel	Stony Point	Rose, Elister	"
Olive, Benjamin	"	Rose, Henry H.	"
Owen, William I	"	Rose, Richard	"
Phillips, John W.	"	Rose, Jacob A.	"
Paul, William H.	"	Rose, Brewster	"
Phillips, Harrison	"	Rose, Calvin	"
Price, William	"	Rose, John R.	"
Penny, Fred., Attorney	"	Rose, Walter	"
Phillips, Thos.	"	Rose, Wilmer	"
Phillips, John W., Jr.	"	Rose, James H.	"

Rose, E. O., Store.....Stony Point	Stalter, Jacob..........Stony Point
Rose, Henry, Jr......... "	Smith, J. J., Rev...Tompkin's Cove
Rose, Nelson............ "	Timothy, Frank....... Stony Point
Rose, Paul............. "	Theill, Matthew.. ...... "
Rose, Peter............ "	Thorpe, Cornelius.......Jones' Point
Rose, Thomas W........ "	Ten Eyck, Allison, Jr.... "
Rose, Wm. A........... "	Ten Eyck, Edwin.......Stony Point
Rose, William .... "	Ten Eyck, Charles...Tompkin's Cove
Rose, Alexander.. ..... "	Tompkins, Watson.. ....Stony Point
Rose, Newman.......... "	Ten Eyck, Alfred...Tompkin's Cove
Rose, David W......... "	Ten Eyck, John.........Stony Point
Rose, William H........ "	Ten Eyck, Thomas......Jones' Point
Rose, Warner........... "	Thompson, John........Stony Point
Rose, Milton.... . .... "	Thompson, E A., Mason "
Rose, William A.. Jr.... "	Tomlins, William....Tompkin's Cove
Rose, Edward.......... "	Tomlins, Newton.... "
Rose, Abram........... "	Tompkins, Calvin.... "
Rose, Alonzo.....Dutchess Junction	Thorne, Robert.........Stony Point
Ryan, William.........Grassy Point	Termansen, Lawritz..... "
Rhodes, George.... .....Jones' Point	Thorne, Albert.......... "
Roderman, —.......Tompkin's Cove	Toole, John... .... "
Rose, Albert............Stony Point	Van Wort, John W...... "
Riker, John............ "	Van Valer, John K...... "
Reiley, Patrick......... . "	Valentine, Benj. C... ...Garnerville
Reiley, Michael......... "	Van Wort, Arthur......Stony Point
Ryder, Egbert.......... "	Vredenburg, Peter....... "
Ryder, William......... "	Vredenberg, Charles..... "
Stalter, James K........ "	Van Wart, Augustus.Tompkin's Cove
Shair, Conrad.......... "	Van Wart, Calvin.....Stony Point
Sillsbury, Archie... ...Grassy Point	Van Wart, Theodore.... "
Springsteed, Geo........Stony Point	Ward, John............Grassy Point
Springsteed, Edw'd..Tompkin's Cove	Wheeler, George........ "
Stalter, Elbert......... Stony Point	Waldron, Belden.......Stony Point
Springsteed, W. A...... "	Wiles, Frank..........Grassy Point
Smalley, Samuel........ "	Wood, William.........Stony Point
Stalter, Nathaniel...... "	Ward, Edward.........Grassy Point
Stalter, John........... "	Ward, George.......... "
Stalter, R. B., Store..... "	Ward, Irving.......... "
Springsteed, Jacob...... "	Williams, Wesley......Stony Point
Springsteed, Joseph..... "	Wright, Charles......... "
Springsteed, Samuel..... "	Weyant, William........ "
Stalter, Nicholas........ "	Weyant, Hiram......... "
Springsteed, Wm... Tompkin's Cove	Waters, John........... "
Springsteed, George.. "	Waters, James......... "
Secor, Josiah B......... ....Thiells	Welch, Andrew......... "
Secor, Samuel....... Stony Point	Wood, William........ . "
Smith, John............ "	Wood, George......... "
Smith, John............ "	Weyant, E. B.......... "
Skerry, William........ "	Wood, Christie.........Stony Point
Scannell, Howard.......Jones' Point	Watkins, Augustus......Jones' Point
Scannell, Isaac.......... "	Watkins, Ishmael....... "
Searing, Walter T...Tompkin's Cove	Watkins, James........ "

Waldron, Resolvert	Stony Point	Wilcox, Stephen	Stony Point
Waldron, Washington	Haverstraw	Wiles, Charles J.	"
Weiant, Wolsey T.	Stony Point	Washburn, U. F.	"
Weiant, Geo. B.	"	Williamson, George	Tompkin's Cove
Whalen, Gregory	Grassy Point	Wicks, George L.	Grassy Point
Weiant, Geo. W., Att'ny	Haverstraw	Washburn, Mordicai	Stony Point
Wiles, William H.	Stony Point	Washburn, Lucien	"
Wright, William	"	Wood, David G.	"
Wiles, Alfred M.	"	Young, John	"
West, James Garner	Haverstraw	Young, Lewis	"
Winter, George	Grassy Point	Young, Charles	"
Weiant, James	Jones' Point	Young, William	"
Wood, George S.	Tompkin's Cove		

CHAPTER VII.

BIOGRAPHICAL SKETCHES.

THE biographic sketches in connection with the names of some of the citizens are samples of the sketches which it was the purpose of the Author to make, but, owing to the fact that persons did not fill the blanks sent them, but few of the people have been thus recorded. The alphabetical list appended will be of great value for a number of purposes.

We think the plan of recording families, as indicated in the following brief outline, is suggestive at least, and we indulge the hope that the work of the Author, or some such method, to preserve the genealogy of the people, will be carried to completion by some one in the near future.

GEORGE ASKEW.

for 18 years one of our leading public instructors, is the son of James Askew, of England. His grandfather was named George. His mother was Carolina L., the daughter of George W. Burr, of Philadelphia. Mr. Askew's children are James, George, Alpha L., Carrie B. (Frank, deceased), Ambrose A., Harry G., Laura G. and Edith E. He is, at present, under a good salary in the

United States service, as storekeeper in the Custom House—Republican and a member of the Episcopal Church.

BREWSTER J. ALLISON,

the son of Judge George S. Allison, was born July 5th, 1821. He spent his early years in school, and, after completing his education, entered business with his father, at first in a store and afterwards in the manufacture of brick. For a time he was also engaged in land surveying. He is a large land owner, and has held many important offices in the town and county. He was member of the Legislature in 1850. At present he is engaged extensively in the brick industry, and in superintending his personal and landed estate. He is a man of remarkable business tact and integrity, and noted for his liberality.

CHARLES ALLISON,

native of Tompkin's County, N. Y.; born Dec. 16, 1838; dealer in sand; son of William Allison, of Haverstraw, and Ruth Bradbury; grandfather, Benjamin, son of Michael Allison; brother's name, John Wesley Allison; second wife, Susie Terwilliger, daughter of John R. Terwilliger. His family consists of two children, Melissa by first wife and Clarence by second wife. Son-in-law, John Jones, father of one child named Bertha. Mr. Allison adheres to the Methodist Church, and is a Republican in politics.

GRASSY POINT, LOOKING EAST.

HANFORD BARTON,

a butcher by trade, was born at Cornwall, Orange County, Feb.

20, 1832, and is the son of Gilbert C. Barton and grandson of Roger Barton, of the same county. His mother was Ann P. Ryer; his brothers and sisters were William, Alanson, Charles, Mary and Adaline. Mr. Barton married Martha, the daughter of James Hazard, Feb. 10, 1864, and the children living are Ella M., Emma J. and Bertha. James is the son of a former wife. Mr. Barton is a Republican, and belongs to the Methodist Episcopal Church.

STONY POINT AVENUE, LOOKING WEST.

LOUIS BOWER,

an experienced moulder in Wiles' manufactory, is the son of John Bower (deceased), and was born Sept. 15, 1852. His mother was Elizabeth Boldauf. Both parents are natives of Germany. The brothers and sisters of Mr. Bower are John, George, Charles, David, Catharine, Elizabeth, Carrie and Amelia. March 3rd, 1875, Mr. Bower married Miss Cassie, daughter of Jacob Dinsdorf (deceased). The living children of these parents are John J. and Willis D. Bower. Mr. Bower is a Methodist.

ALEX. S. BULSON,

a boat captain of great experience, and one of the most worthy citizens, was born April 13, 1821. His father's name was John, and his grandfather's, Alax. His great-grandfather was a native of Holland, and assisted in the erection of the first church in New York city, the brick and tiling having been brought from Holland. His mother was Catherine Dykens, and was French. The name of Mrs. Bulson is Martha, the daughter of Andrew Rose. The children are John, Edgar, Henry, Edmund and Dora. The grandchildren are Alonzo, Mattie, William, Edith, Martha, Alfred, and Eva K. (deceased.)

WM. B. CAVEL

was born Sept. 14, 1860, in the town of Marquette, Mich. His father, Wm. Cavel, died in the late war. Mr. Cavel is a telegraph operator, and at present engaged in keeping a meat market on corner of Hudson Street and Stony Point Avenue.

JAMES CONKLIN,

a man of sterling moral and business integrity, commenced life without means, and is now, in good circumstances, residing at Dutchess Junction. Mr. Conklin was early connected with the history of the Methodist Episcopal Church. His wife was Miss Charlotte Knapp, the daughter of Colonel Robert Knapp. Mrs. Conklin is one of nine children, and of a family widely known.

ALONZO DYKENS,

a clerk in the store of D. Tomkins & Sons, is the son of Abraham Dykens. He was born Feb. 19, 1854. His father was born November 14, 1826; and his mother, Nancy McLary, was born January 4, 1826. The brothers of Alonzo are George W. and Edgar (deceased). Mr. Dykens was married to Miss Elma C., the daughter of James B. Hoyt, Dec. 31, 1879. The children's names are Elma C. and Susie Dykens. Republican in politics; church, Methodist Episcopal.

DR. N. GARRISON

is a practising physician of the town. By careful attention to business he has acquired considerable estate. His residence is one mile north of the village of Stony Point. He has an extended practice, having traveled the same parish for thirty years. His father, an eminent practitioner, preceded him here.

WM. E. GARRISON,

native of Fort Montgomery, born April 7, 1818—son of James Garrison and Elizabeth House. Mr. Garrison is a sailor by profession, and has been a life-long resident of this county. His grandfather, Isaac Garrison, lived at Quenmans, near Albany, and his great-grandfather came from Low Dutch. His grandmother, Elizabeth Koofort, also of Dutch descent.

He had but one brother and no sister. Brother's name, Moses; dead three years. Wife's name, Elizabeth Cronk. Family consists of Elizabeth, Emily, Martha and Mary Ann; son-in-law, George I.; grandchild, Addie Georgia I. He adheres to the Episcopal Church, and a Democrat in politics. Mr. Garrison has furnished a short sketch as tradition.

JAS. H. HAZARD,

born Orange Co., Aug. 15, 1837, is a butcher by trade. His father is James Hazard; his grandfather was James, and his grandmother's name was Martha Gould, of Blackrock, Conn., of English descent; his mother's maiden name was Sarah Cornell, a relative of Gov. Cornell; the grandmother, on mother's side, was Elleanor Hunt. His brothers are Benjamin and William Daniel. Neither of them ever " smoked, chewed, or drank." His wife's name was (Emma) Weiley, daughter of James Weiley, of Cornwall. They were married Nov. 18, 1863. Their children are Mary, Alice, Lizzie, Robert and William. Republican, adheres to Friends (Quakers).

WM. F. HOLT,

a shopkeeper and confectioner on Stony Point Avenue, was born in New York city, and is the son of Thomas P. Holt (deceased), who was a native of Ontario and born 1824. His grandparents were B. F. Goodspeed, of New York city, and Alma Parker; his brothers are Albert M., Thomas and Edwin. Prohibitionist; Methodist Episcopal Church.

CHAS. S. HARRISON,

an extensive furniture dealer in Jersey City, born in Kent, Eng.,

STONY POINT ILLUSTRATED.

STONY POINT AVENUE, LOOKING EAST.

February 7, 1837, is the son of John, who was born in Norwich, March 10, 1802, and the grandson of Charles Harrison of the same place in England, the birth of the latter being 1756. Mr. Harrison's mother was Sarah Parker, of Canterbury; one of the grandmothers was a Scofield, born in Norwich, Eng., April 7, 1777. The brothers are John, George and Henry; the sisters, Sarah and Elizabeth; children of Mr. Harrison, by first marriage, are Charles, John, William and Alice; daughters-in-law, Kate and Francina; the grand-children are Charles, Mabel, Ella, May. The second marriage, to Miss Abbie H., daughter of Peter Lyke, occurred July 4, 1883. Prohibitionist; adherent Methodist Episcopal Church.

JOHN A. HELVIN,

a native of Prince George County, Va., was born June 10, 1847. His father was G. W. Helvin, who was born in Sussex Co., Va., Sept. 22, 1818, and was the son of an Englishman by name of George Thadeous Helvin. The great-grandfather's name was also George. No record remains of the locality of the birth of the two last named.

Mr. Helvin's mother, Harriet R. Perkins, who still resides with him in Haverstraw, was the daughter of Lucy Clayton Perkins, and was born in Dinwiddie Co., Va., Aug. 13, 1818, her mother, Lucy Clayton, having been born in the same county, Oct. 22, 1789. Mr. Helvin's great-grandmother was Ann Robertson Kirby, of Brunswick Co., Va. The brothers of Mr. John H. Helvin are James F. and George W., and his sister is Lucy Ann. Mrs. J. H. Helvin was Miss Martha L., daughter of Samuel P. Foster, and took the hand of Mr. Helvin, March 15, 1871. The children are Alfred Lee, Gracie R., Mamie, Nellie, Ernest, Leslie, and Jas. Herbert. Prohibitionist and Methodist in earnest.

JAS. R. HAMMOND,

a contractor and mason, has a liberal education, is a good clerk, and is succeeding in business. He resides in his own house near West Shore, West Haverstraw. He is a brother of William K. Hammond, and the son of Edmond J. Hammond and Rachel Knapp. He married Phoebe, the daughter of Oscar Wood, Nov. 30, 1882. He is identified with the M. E. Church, being one of its honored and faithful supporters.

DANIEL HAZARD,

a successful butcher of the place, was born in Orange Co., April 17, 1844, is the son of James Hazard and the brother of Benjamin, William and James. His sisters are Mary W., Charlotte C., Elenor, Martha and Sarah Jane. His wife, Augusta H., whom he married Aug. 30, 1865, was the daughter of Foster D. Birdsall and Mary Ann Young. The sons of Mr. and Mrs. Hazard are George B., deceased, and Frank Foster, who is in business with his father. Republican, voted Prohibition; brought up Quaker; attends M. E. Church.

ABRAHAM HURD,

an experienced brick maker and foreman, was born Nov. 13, 1838, and is the son of Wm. Hurd and the grandson of John Hurd. His mother was Catharine Odell. His grandmother, Ruth Conley, of Orange County. His brother and sisters are Wm. Hurd, Adelia March and Catharine Wood. His wife's name was Ann, the daughter of John C. Miller. The marriage of Mr. and Mrs. Hurd is dated Oct. 24, 1860; their children are Matthew, Wm. J., David, Sarah and Carrie. Republican; P. Methodist.

ADDISON JOHNSON,

deceased, was born in the town of Haverstraw, Jan. 20, 1844, and married Adelia, the daughter of Wm. Hurd, March 29, 1862. His father was Charles and his grandfather James Johnson; his mother's maiden name was Fanny Adams; his brothers are Harrison, Walter and Wesley; the sisters, Louise and Abigail. Mr. Johnson's children are Cassie, Agnes and Charles. Miss Agnes married Samuel Blauvelt. The grandchildren are Lillian M. and Edward Blauvelt. The politics of Mr. Johnson were Republican. He was a member of the M. E. Church.

WM. J. JONES,

born in Hempstead, Rockland Co., N. Y., and is about 69 years of age. His father was John B. and grandfather Benjamin Jones. The mother of Mr. Jones was Gersiah Odell, of Canterbury, Orange Co.; the brothers are Alfred, Clinton, Benjamin; the sisters, Sally, Ann, Betsy, Emeline and Rebecca. He married Abigail, daughter of Abraham Jones, July 5, 1847; the children are Daniel, Wm. L., Benjamin, Susan, Rebecca, Emeline; sons-in-law, Wm. Yeomans, Ed. Hoyt. Democrat.

DANIEL KEESLER

was born in Newark, N. J., July 25, 1839. His trade is that of house, sign and ornamental painter, and keeps supplies for house furnishing, hardware, etc. His mother's maiden name Mary E. Guiler; her birthplace was Amsterdam, Germany; she is a woman of rare intellect and business capacity. The sisters of Daniel are Julia, Mary, Margaret and Elizabeth. Mr. Keesler was married to Miss Eliza A., daughter of Nicholas Stalter, July 3d, 1860. The children are H. Louisa, Lizzie, Edward D., Freddie and Harry. In politics Prohibitionist, and a Presbyterian.

KNAPP

is German. Albert Knapp, the German poet, was a native of Wurtemburg, Germany. Chauncey L. Knapp, editor of the Vermont *State Journal*, held many prominent positions of State. Geo. Christian Knapp was a German Theologian, and an author of "Lectures on Theology." Jacob Knapp was a second Moody, having, during 12 years, made 100,000 converts to religion.

John Knapp, son of Abraham Knapp, was the son of Lebius, who was a native of Horseneck, Conn. Mr. Knapp was born July 17, 1810. He followed the butcher business for 30 years. His brothers are Samuel, Henry and Levi; the sisters are Rachel, Elizabeth and Adelia. Mr. Knapp enjoys a comfortable income, and is remarkably vigorous for a man of his age.

COL. ROBERT KNAPP

was a man of some note in Rockland. He died Feb. 19, 1859, aged 65 years. His military career extended to a command of the Regiment of Rockland County. At his funeral the Stony Point Guards turned out in a body. His funeral sermon was preached by Rev. F. S. Wolf, pastor of the Creek Church.

JOHN P. LINKLETTER,

a native of Stony Point, born Aug. 29, 1836; son of George J. Linkletter, born at Haverstraw, Sept. 5, 1795, and Rachel Weiant, also of Haverstraw, born April 11, 1799. His grandparents were John Linkletter and Susan Vanhorne, both of Ramapo; great-grandfather probably Scotch; his brothers names are William and George, brothers to Catherine, Martha and Mary Elizabeth. He married Emma Knowlton, daughter of James Knowlton, Jan. 12, 1858; his family consists of two sons, James K. and William R.; he has one daughter-in-law, Cassie Hoyt, and one grandchild, Pearl. He adhere to the Methodist Church, and is a Republican Prohibitionist.

ISAAC N. LEMMON,

born at Mt. Pleasant, Ohio, July 24, 1851. Mr. Lemmon is a farmer by profession, and has a family consisting of two children, Mary Adella and Catherine Estella. He married Rebecca A. June, daughter of Ethiel June, in Sept., 1872. His ancestors were—father, Moses Lemmon, born in Harrison Co., Ohio, 1818; grandfather, Jacob Lemmon; great-grandfather, Abraham Lem-

RESIDENCES ON STONY POINT AVENUE.

mon; mother, Mary Ann Allen, born in Harrison Co., Ohio; grandmother, Mary Marquhart, born in Virginia in 1785. His brothers' names are Allen B., William, Chas. S. and Edgar, with one sister, Clara. Independent Republican in politics.

JOHN T. LEACH,

of Wellingham, Cambridgeshire, England, a skillful mechanic and woodworker in the extensive machine manufactory of A. M. & W. H. Wiles, was born Nov. 5th, 1832. His father was Richard Leach, of the same place, and his mother's name was Ruth Fen, also of Wellingham. The brothers of Mr. Leach are Charles and Elijah; the sisters, Eliza, Lizzie and Anna. July 2, 1860, he married Martha, the daughter of James Miller. His children are Charles R. L., Martha E., George A., Frederick J., Frank, Maggie and Sarah. Martha E. married Charles Convoy. Politics, Republican; church, Presbyterian.

JEREMIAH MERRITT

was born at Monroe, Orange Co., N. Y., June 25th, 1836. He is a blacksmith and an anthracite furnaceman. His father's name was Abraham; his grandfather's name was Jeremiah; his great-grandfather's name was Abraham; his mother was Elizabeth Conklin, daughter of Elizabeth Odell, of Orange Co., N. Y.; his brothers are Abram, Peter D., William, Samuel and Charles; sisters, Caroline, Sarah and Alice, two of whom are deceased. He married Lucy Ann, daughter of Isaac Coe, July 3rd, 1857; his children are Sarah J., Mary M., Martha A., Francis D., Emma V., Libbie, Annie A., Wm. H.; sons-in-law, Wm. A. Dare, Jas. Hillard, Wm. Quelch, Joseph Washburn, Daniel Barton, and William Allen, deceased.

ABRM. D. MARKS,

born Westchester Co., March 19, 1822; painter; son of Moses I. Marks, of Sing Sing, 1792; his mother's name was Rebecca Clark, who was born in Delaware, 1794. He married Jane V., daughter of Benj. Colter, April, 1841, and has children, viz., Anna, Richard and Adaline; sons-in-law, Joseph F. Umpleby and Geo. W. Farmer. Politics, Republican; church, Presbyterian

Enlisted in late war, Aug. 29, 1861. In battles on Potomac, Hancock, Bolivier Heights, Charleston, Slaughter Mountain, on the Rapahannock; in Libby and Belle Island Prisons 37 days; with the writer in Chancellorville, May 1, 2, and 3, where he lay wounded on the field 12 days; in hospital 11 months; discharged, April 3, 1864; Sept., 1877, had a ball taken from his side, having carried it, under much suffering, for 14 years. He is worthily pensioned.

RESIDENCE OF MR. R. B. MARKS.

R. B. MARKS

was born July 12, 1830; he is the son of Alfred Marks, who was born at Peekskill; the grandfather of R. B. was Michael, of London, Eng.; the mother of Mr. Marks was Mary Brewster, a native of Stony Point, and descended from one of the first families of the Revolutionary days; a grandmother's maiden name was Johaveth Isaacs, of Connecticut. Mr. Marks married Miss Catherine Marks, the daughter of Sampson Marks, Nov. 12, 1851; the children are Charles and George, who are in business here, and

Annie J., the wife of Sidney Witkowsky, resident and in mercantile business, Chicago, Ill. Mr. George married Estelle Lent, and Charles, Miss Johannah Ossman. The grandchild is Annie J. Mr. Marks has done valuable services as overseer of the poor and commissioner in the county.

WALTER M. MC BRIDE,

son of Walter McBride, was born in New York city, March 27, 1824; his grandparents were from Virginia; brothers, Andrew Jackson McBride and George Washington McBride; he married Amelia, daughter of David Johnson, in 1847; the children's names are Elizabeth, Susan and Walter; son-in-law, George M. Raymond. M. E. Church, and is a Prohibitionist.

WM. L. OWENS,

born at Newburg, June 18, 1828, and is the son of Jonathan Owens, who was born June 28, 1786, and grandson of James. Mr. Owens' mother was Elizabeth, the daughter of Keriah Innis, of Scotland, and born Oct. 12, 1766. The brothers were Reuben H. and Jas. H.; the sisters, Elizabeth, Catherine H., Sarah L. and Keriza A. Mr. Owens and Miss Rachel A. Phillips, the daughter of James E. Phillips, were joined in marriage Aug. 4, 1849; the names of their children are George S., Susana E., Alsi M. and Justien A. The only survivor is Alsi, who married Miss Annie Babcock; the names of the grandchildren are John M. and Lucretia. Politics, Temperance; church, M. E.

JOHN W. PHILLIPS, SR.,

born April 19, 1831, a boatman by trade, is the son of George Phillips and grandson of Daniel P. Phillips and J. L. Knapp, and great-grandson of Daniel Phillips. His mother's name was Knapp, and grandmother's Hannah Osborn; he married Sarah, daughter of Wm. Hill, Nov. 11th, 1852; the children are Daniel, Hannah, Alonzo and John W.; son-in-law, John W. Webber; grandchildren, Arthur, Harry and Albert. Politics, a Jackson Democrat; Protestant.

JOHN W. PHILLIPS, JR.,

a salesman, son of J. W. Phillips and Sarah Hill, and brother to Daniel and Alonzo, and Hannah. Politics, neutral; Protestant.

WM. PHILLIPS,

born Haverstraw, 1819, butcher, the son of Jas. E., grandson of Eli, and great-grandson of John, of Holland; his mother was Susanna Burd, his grandmother Rachel Halsted; the brothers were Charles, John and Thomas; sisters, Esther, Hannah, Ann Elizabeth, Rachel. His first wife was Maria, daughter of Henry Essex; the second wife, Lizzie Blauvelt. Children by first wife, James, Henry, Mary Ann, Ellen Maria, Selina, George; son-in-law, Jacob Engle, whose son, Willie, is the only grandson of Mr. Phillips. Prohibition (Rep.); adheres to M. E. Church.

ROSE

is from Dutch Rozee, the favorite name of a female. The French word Rozet is pronounced ro-ze'.

ALAX. ROSE,

the son of Alax. Rose and Nancy Springsteed, is a member of the firm of Reilly & Rose, who are successful brick manufacturers. He is a grandson of Jacob Rose, and his great-grandfather was of Revolutionary notoriety; his mother is the faithful keeper of the Lighthouse, and has been so for 34 years; he is a descendant of the Parkerson and Storms families; his sisters are Lavinia and Melinda. Republican; Presbyterian.

WM. A. ROSE,

son of Elester Rose, was born Dec. 10th, 1860, and is the grandson of Moses Marks; his mother's maiden name was Frances M. Marks. Sept. 5th, 1885, Mr. Rose was married to Miss Maggie, the daughter of Nelson Cropman; the name of their child is Helen. Mr. Rose's brothers and sisters are Oscar E., Edwin O., Louis A., Robt. F., Lottie R., and Edith A. Prohibitionist; M. E. Church.

THOMAS REILLY,

born in Ireland in 1843, is the son of James Reilly, who was born in the same country in 1791; his mother's maiden name was Mary Fitzsimmons, born 1806; Phillip, Michael, James, Patrick, Julia and Bridget are his brothers and sisters. Mr. Reilly is in the profitable business of brick making, and forms a part of the firm of Reilly & Clark. Democrat; Rom. Catholic.

WM. ROSE,

brother of James H. Rose, the husband of Catherine E. Linkletter, who was the daughter of George J. Linkletter. The marriage of Mr. Rose occurred April 13, 1847; the children are Ada M. Wanamaker, Laura Ferguson, Arnold B., and Wm. W. Rose; the son-in-law is John Ferguson, children are Willie and Johnnie. Church, M. E.

REV. OLIVER RYDER,

born in Orange County, July 18, 1828; received local preacher's license, 1857; connected with Tompkin's Cove Protestant Methodist Church. He is son of William Ryder, whose father was Jacob, and grandfather's name was Linous; Mr. Ryder's mother's name was Frances J. Clark, of same county, and she was the daughter of Hatherin Potter; the brothers were Jacob, Clark, William; the sisters, Sarah, Jane, Martha. His wife was Mary, daughter of Charles Van Wart; the children are William, Egbert, Oliver, Cecilia, Laura; son-in-law, T. F. Macmannas; daughters-in-law, Josephine and Ida S.; the grandchildren are Lillie, Lulu, George, Edith, Oscar, Oliver B. Prohibitionist.

ALONZO ROSE,

a native, but now residing at Duchess Junction, was born 1840, and is the son of J. H. Rose and Rebecca Knapp. The names of his grandfathers are Henry Rose and Abel Knapp; Mrs. Abbey Phillips was his grandmother. His only brother is Newman; the sisters are Almira Fales, Abby, wife of Capt. Jas. Leet, and Mary. Mr. Rose married Miss Emma J. Wilkins, Nov. 22, 1865; the children born to them are Irving J. and Alonzo K. He is a successful brick manufacturer. The citizens of Stony Point reluctantly parted with the family when they removed to Duchess Junction. Prohibitionist; Methodist.

JAMES ROSE,

born July 4, 1855, is the son of Alfred Rose, who was the son of Henry; his mother's maiden name was Rachel Jones; the grandmother of Mr. Rose was Mary Dykins; the only brother of James is Alfred; the sisters are Anna, Carrie and Minnie. He married

Miss Dora Bulson, the daughter of Alax. J. Bulson; the wedding day was July 4, 1878; the children are Martha, Alfred, Eva K., deceased. Politics, neutral; church, M. E.

NELSON ROSE,

a native of this town, was born in the year 1846—Oct. 27. He is a captain of a schooner, having earned the reputation of a good boatman. He is the son of Henry H. Rose, who was born in 1807; the grandfather was also Henry H., and was the descendant of Jacob Rose, the Revolutionary patriot boy. The maiden name of his mother was Catherine Jones, whose birthday dates back to 1819. Mr. N. Rose and wife, Jane Stalter, were married Feb. 2, 1870; the children born to them are Marvin and Elbert Rose. Prohibitionist, and belongs to the M. E. Church.

WM. H. ROSE,

born at Stony Point, N. Y.; son of William Rose and Rachel Walton. He was at first engaged in the brick industry of our town, and later on abandoned it and became a carriage maker in the metropolis. He has had charge of the Presbyterian Sabbath School about fifteen years, having been absent but one Sabbath, except when kept away by sickness. About five hundred scholars have been connected with the school, and of this number about ninety per cent. are or have been connected in the churches of this or other places. His brothers are Edward, Samuel P., Hiram, Walton and Thomas; sisters, Catherine, Caroline, Phoebe and Elmira; wife, Hannah Rebecca Bourse. His family consists of three children, Miriam, Martha and Sarah Elizabeth. Sons-in-law, Rev. Julius L. Danner and Minott M. Govan; grandchildren, Edgar Wm., Henry Rose, and Julius L. Danner, Jr., Edith, Louise and Jennie Govan. Belongs to the Presbyterian Church, and is a Republican.

WALTER T. SEARING,

a successful merchant, is the son of Warren Searing, a native of Newark, N. J., who was born there July 1st, 1810, being the son of James Searing, of Lyons Farm, N. J. Walter was born at Tompkin's Cove, his residence, July 13, 1846. His mother's name before marriage was Mary Machette, also of Newark, and born Nov. 1st, 1818. The name of one of his grandmother's was Elizabeth Dunham, of Westfield, N. J. Mr. Searing has one brother, Edwin, his sisters being Cornelia, Mary, Laura, Cassie, Cecilia, Anna. First wife was Mintie Kirby, daughter of Daniel Kirby. The marriage to Miss Kirby occurred Sept. 10th, 1868. Second wife was Elizabeth, daughter of Rev. Wm. W. McNair, the wedding day having been May 10, 1876. The last wife has also died recently. The children of Mr. Searing are Esther, Mary, Louise, Mintie and Earnest. Rep.; M. P. Church.

NICHOLAS STALTER,

an experienced brick burner, is the son of Nicholas Stalter, who was a native of Nova Scotia. His mother was Rachel Baisley, the daughter of Wm. Baisley. The brother of Mr. Stalter is Brewster; his sister's name is Catherine. The present wife, whom he married Feb. 3, 1864, is the daughter of Mr. Bulson. The children by his first wife are Eliza, the wife of D. Keesler; Theodore, Amelia, Brewster, Jane, the wife of Nelson Rose; R. B., the storekeeper, and Elbert. An only son of the last wife is Fred. There are three sons-in-law, five daughters-in-law, and 21 grand children. In politics, Democrat; church adherent, Methodist Episcopal.

RICHARD B. STALTER,

native of Stony Point, born Jan. 12, 1852. Mr. Stalters' parents were Nicholas, son of Nicholas Stalter and Hannah Brewster, both of Stony Point, N. Y. His brothers' names are Theodore Brewster, Elbert and Freddie; sisters, Eliza A., Margaret, Jane and Amelia. He took the hand of Abbie, daughter of William Cosgrove, in marriage April 29, 1872; their four children are Maud, Hattie, Walter and Jennie. Mr. Staltar is a merchant of our village, and a Democrat in politics; and a Presbyterian.

JOHN TEN EYCK

resides on Stony Point, overlooking King's Ferry. He was born Jan. 22, 1814, and was the son of David Ten Eyck. His mother's maiden name was Elizabeth Babcock. One of his grandmothers was an Allison. His brothers are Thomas and James; sister, Harriet Gains. He married Sept. 24, 1846, Hannah W., the daughter of Lewis Constant. Mr. Ten Eyck has had the advantage of travel and extensive observation. Has a good memory; is a son of one of the early settlers. A Republican; Protestant.

LAURITZ TERMANSEN,

born in Denmark, July 12, 1847. He is an extensive house decorator, doing business in New York city. His father's name is Lauritzen, the grandfather and great-grandfather bearing the same name. Mr. Termansen's mother was Amy Larsen, the daughter of Karen Neilsen, the daughter of Amy Mortensen. The brother and sister of Mr. Termansen are Peter and Karen Termansen, all of Denmark. Mrs. Leine Termansen is the daughter of Conrad Young, deceased, their marriage having taken place April 20, 1878. The child's name is Clare Adeline. In politics, Independent; Presbyterian Church.

WATSON TOMKINS

is a native of Newark, N. J.; born May 5th, 1829. He is the son of Daniel Tomkins, and considered one of the representative business men of our town. His father first settled at Tompkin's Cove, and it was here that Watson began his business career. A few years later he engaged in the manufacture of brick, and is now the possessor of valuable clay beds along the beach. It was through his influence and zeal for the welfare of the public that our beautiful West Shore Station was built. He gives employment to a large number of men, and is a man of generous impulses.

HON. WESLEY J. WEIANT,

deceased, was born in 1811, and was of French and German extraction. He was the son of George Weiant and Catherine Waldron, his father having died in the year 1855. In 1836 he married Miss Catherine Rose, daughter of Jacob, the son of the Revolutionary Jacob Rose, a sketch of whose experience we have preserved. Mr. Weiant was intimately acquainted with the affairs of the public, and served as supervisor in 1857 and was elected to the Legislature of New York in 1859, where he served on important committees and made an address which produced a profound impression. He was a man of more than ordinary legal mind, and was an able man in address in the various services in the M. E. Church, to which he was zealously attached for many years. He died during the summer of 1886 from an accident of falling from a tree. His fine property, now occupied by the widow, is offered for sale. An engraving of it appears in one of our groups.

SAM'L P. WOOD,

a carpenter, the son of Jacob Wood of Westchester Co., was born in this town. His mother's name was Mary Peterson, also of Westchester. One of the grandparents was Francis Walker, who was born in Grantham, England, in 1789. The brothers of Mr. Wood are Benj. F., Wm. E., Geo. A.; the sisters are Sarah F., Lucinda and Mary E. Prohibition and Methodist.

E. B. WEIANT,

painter, born Sept. 29, 1843. Jan. 29, 1867, he was married to Miss Maggie L. Stephens, the daughter of Stephen Stephens, an Englishman. The living children of Mr. Weiant are Elizabeth, Eva L., Violetta and Gerald Edward. Mr. Weiant served in the late war; received injuries, from which he has suffered, and on which account he is now a pensioner. He is in active relation with the M. E. Church, and Sunday School superintendent. Republican and Prohibition.

SPENCER J. WEIANT,

born Dec. 6, 1864, is the son of Spencer J. and grandson of Abrm. Weiant, and great-grandson of Geo. Weiant. His mother's name was Annie E. Van Pelt; his grandmother and great-grandmother were Clarisa Weiant and Mary Hazard, both of Orange Co. His brothers are Alfred and Frank. Mr. Weiant is a successful railroad clerk in the employ of the great West Shore.

GEO. L. WICKS,

an enterprising boat builder at Grassy Point, is the son of Geo. L. Wicks and Clarsie Thing, all of Long Island. Mr. Wicks was

GRASSY POINT, LOOKING WEST.

born Feb. 16, 1846. His grandfather was Robt. L. and great-grandfather Lewis Wicks. They were English. The brothers of Mr. Wicks are Thomas W. and Wm. Wicks; the sisters, Mary and Alice. His second marriage was Jan. 2, 1873, to Henrietta L., the daughter of John Mahan. The surviving children are Lucy, Ella and Geo. L. Wicks. Independent; a member of the M. E. Church.

ALFRED M. WILES,

born in London, England, Jan. 13, 1829. His father was John J. Wiles, and his mother Ann M. Kames; she was born February 3, 1796. The brothers and sisters are Joseph K., Wm. H., Frederick J., Elizabeth, Emma S. and Harriet. Mr. Wiles married Miss Catherine, the daughter of Jacob Blauvelt, Nov. 26, 1853. The children are Rhoda A., Edwin L. and Maggie. Mr. Wiles is popularly known as the head of the firm known as A. M. & W. H. Wiles. Their manufactory is without a peer in their line. A Democrat.

W. H. WILES,

of the firm of A. M. & W. H. Wiles, is a brother of Alfred M., whose birth and ancestry will explain his. Mr. Wiles is a genius and well read, as is his brother Alfred. In the year 1850, Aug. 11, Wm. Wiles married Mary E., the daughter of Jacob Fredrick.

The children are John J., Fredrick J., Mary S., Francis E., Lydia A., Martha L., Emma L. and Fannie J. The sons-in-law are the Hon. Alonzo Wheeler and David R. Wadsworth; daughters-in-law, M. Clara Hazard, Kate M. Brooks, Mary B. Rose; the grandchildren are Jeanie S., Jessie L., Ethel M., Jay B. and Florence A. Democrat; Presbyterian.

CHAS. J. WILES,

born April 8, 1846, at Balmville, near Newburgh; by profession a pattern maker, employed at Wiles. He is the son of Jos. K. Wiles and Elizabeth Thomas. His father is English; his mother a native of Orange Co. The grandfather was John J. Wiles. His sisters are Eliza J., Mary E., Ella and Hattie. His marriage to Miss Adelia B., daughter of W. F. B. Gurnee, occurred Oct. 10, 1873. The children are Joseph K., Ella B. and Susie D. Republican; adheres to Pres. Church. (See cut of house.)

CHAPTER VIII.

SELF-MADE MEN.

J. J. SMITH, M. A., D. D.,

PASTOR of the Tompkin's Cove Methodist Protestant Church, is spending a fourth term of pastorate with his present church, making in all eleven years.

Mr. Smith is a man of literary attainments, and has written extensively on travel and science. He was elected, without his knowledge, a member of "The American Institute of Christian Philosophy," in New York. The high honor of his election was on account of his writings, which appeared from time to time in the *Scientific Arena*.

More recently he was officially notified of his having been

elected, for the same reason, to a Fellowship in the Society of Science, Letters and Art of London.

He was born in Atlantic Co., N. J., Feb. 3d, 1817. Converted Sept. 10, 1832, and joined his present denomination. He was licensed May 9th, 1835, and joined the Itineracy in 1836. Has been a member of his Conference 48 years, and its president altogether over 9 years. He represented his Conference in General Conference and Conventions 12 different times. He appeared among the fraternal delegates in the General Conference of the Methodist Episcopal Church in Cincinnatti, 1880. He has been an honored Trustee of Adrian College since 1866. In 1884 the Doctor was elected to a Professorship in Florida University, but preferred the regular ministry.

WILLIAM GOVAN, A. M., M. D.,

was born at Barnet, in Vermont, August 12th, 1818. His father, Andrew, son of William Govan, was a native of Scotland, and came to America about 1815. His mother was Jane, the daughter of Robert Stark. His early years were spent in striving for an education. A graduate of Dartmouth College in 1839, he afterwards received the degree of M. D. from the New York Medical College in 1854, and soon after came to Stony Point, the chosen field of his life-work. He has held many worthy offices in both town and county, and is a member of several Medical Societies. He is at present a member of the Rockland County Historical Association and President of the Board of Education here. He married Lucia J. Mitchell, the daughter of Chauncey R. Mitchell, late of Peekskill, N. Y. Their children have been two sons and a daughter.

WM. K. HAMMOND,

the subject of this sketch, was born in the town of Haverstraw. His father, Edmund J., who was born in 1822 at Croton, Westchester Co., and died when William K. was young. At 10 years of age young William engaged to work for a farmer. The following season he followed boating, and worked on the brick yard one year later. Seeing the business qualities in the boy, his uncle,

Wm. R. Knapp, took him into his store at Knight's Corner. By the recommendation of Wm. R. Knapp, Mr. Hammond received a situation with the firm of Hoagland & Bell, No. 330 West Street, New York, where he remained six years, and having received their confidence, was promoted to a managing clerkship of the firm. He was then sent for by the firm of Candee, Smith & Co., which was at that time the largest mercantile firm in the building material business in New York city. With this company he remained two years.

In 1873 Mr. Hammond married Miss Elizabeth C. Taylor, the daughter of Wm. Taylor and Elizabeth Craig, of New York city.

Wm. R. Knapp, having established in New York city a large agency for the sale of brick, employed Mr. Hammond, with the express understanding that he should become a partner in the business at the end of the year. Before the close of the year Mr. Knapp died, and the aspiring young man returned home with sad prospects; but Mr. Knapp's partners continuing the business, retained Mr. Hammond. But, through improper methods of business, the firm came to ruin in less than eighteen months, when, the consignees of the goods, knowing the business qualities and integrity of the clerk, arranged at once with him, and Mr. Hammond began business for himself in 1875, in which he has continued until the present.

The secret of his success is that in early childhood he obeyed his mother, who faithfully taught him the value of economizing every hour in the attainment of a preparation for business. He, during the period of his clerkship in New York, attended an evening high school, where he took up mathematics, bookkeeping and Latin. Mr. Hammond is a great reader. In 1878 Judge Shandley, and others connected with Tammany Hall, desired him to accept the nomination for Senator of his district in New York city. Although nomination was sure to be an election, he had his own reasons for declining. In his own native town he was elected supervisor, being re-elected without opposition the second time.

Mr. Hammond is greatly interested in the moral and mental

improvement of the young people, and in 1886 organized a Lyceum in St. George's Church, with the following by-laws: "The objects of this association are to improve and cultivate the Sunday School of the St. George's M. E. Church of Stony Point, N. Y.; to foster acquaintances and promote friendships; to reform abuses of criticism, or gossip; to acquire, preserve and disseminate valuable information pertaining to Sunday schools, literary societies and such further matter as will tend to the improvement of the minds of the youth of this community."

HON. SAMUEL HARRISON EVERETT.

Among the men of note of the present day who have sprung from sturdy Putnam County stock, none has carved out for himself a more noble record than the gentleman described in these pages. Mr. Everett was born in the town of Carmel, April 3rd, 1836. When he started in life on his own account, his capital consisted of correct habits, untiring industry, a will that scorned reverses, and the sum of thirteen cents. He made fortune after fortune during his lifetime, and lost them through no fault of his own; but this did not dampen his spirits, and to-day he is a large real estate owner and derives a heavy income from his business. His ancestors, who came from Scotland about the middle of the seventeenth century, were among the early settlers in America. They landed on Long Island in the year 1746, and soon after some of the family effected a permanent settlement in Carmel, Putnam County. Before the Revolutionary War, Isaac Everett, a mason by trade, was engaged in building blast furnaces. The record in Putnam County shows that his ancestors had early become large real estate owners in a district that was constantly improving. Abraham Everett had five sons, Charles, Amos, Samuel, Leonard and Abraham. The family were the pioneers in the Western cattle trade, and drove their fatted steers to market long before railroads were built. Charles was the eldest son and the father of Samuel II. Soon after young Samuel was born, he moved to the south-east and purchased 105 acres of land, which he continued to add to until he acquired an extensive territory. He had four sons,

Oscar, Samuel Harrison, Charles Edwin, Francis Henry, and seven daughters. At a very young age Samuel showed great ambition, and at eleven years was able to cope with the workmen on his father's farm. He went to the district school in winter and worked on the farm in summer, and at the age of eighteen entered Raymond College, where he pursued a course of two years study, under the presidency of Rev. H. G. Livingston. Severe studying injured his health, and he returned home to the farm, where he quickly recuperated. Yearning for a wider field of action, he turned his face to the Metropolis. When he left the homestead, his mother tenderly embracing him, said, " God speed you, Samuel." He had $36 in money when he left, but when he came to face life in New York, he had nothing but the capital mentioned at the opening of this sketch. His heart never failed him, and soon he was master of a rich bank account. Disaster overtook him in the inclement weather of 1862, and his business was literally ruined. The stroke fell with severer force, for he had then become a husband and father. His wife was Margaret, daughter of James Percival, and their eldest daughter was Ida Bell Everett. He accepted an engagement as hotel clerk for himself and family, and four years later his second daughter, Evelyn Percival Everett, was born. Both of these daughters are graduates of Drew Seminary at Carmel.

He sustained a severe blow on March 12th, 1870, in the loss of his affectionate wife. Her father proved his benefactor, and loaned him $6,000, with which he purchased the old People's Hotel at 106 Vesey Street. He speedily transformed it into a first-class hotel, and finished the grand dining room in a style equal to any in the city. The Everett Hotel now occupies parts of nine city lots, and extends from Vesey to Barclay Street. They were purchased in fee simple for $450,000, and the chief ownership is in Mr. Everett, who is conducting a hotel business second to none in the city.

Mr. Everett is not selfish; he lives to do good to others and to better the world. He served for five years as a school trustee for the Third Ward of this city, and resigned to take a seat in the

Assembly as the representative of his native county. His labors in Albany in the Winter of 1881 for the protection of the Putnam County lakes, and for procuring a plentiful supply of pure water for New York, are too well known to require recapitulation here. He took an active part in the defeat of Roscoe Conkling and Thomas C. Platt, who resigned their seats in the United States Senate and sought to be again returned for their vindication. Although a Republican, he persistently voted against them, and remained in his seat fifty-six consecutive days for that purpose. He declined the Republican nomination for a second term for the Assembly, but, under the pressure brought to bear by his friends, he accepted the nomination for State Senator for the Fourteenth District. He made an unequaled run, being beaten by but 208 votes, his opponent being the Hon. Horner A. Nelson, a popular and well-known Democrat. Recently, on account of a large business, he has taken no active part in politics.

Mr. Everett is now president of the Board of Trustees of the Rev. T. De Witt Talmage's Tabernacle. His gifts to the poor and the church are munificent.

His present wife is the daughter of A. H. Todd, of Katonah, N. Y., and is the mother of two sons, Samuel H., Jr., and Chas. E. (2nd), and one daughter, Susan Mary. Mr. Everett is tall and of wiry and athletic build, with dark, but benevolent features. The record of his life is a chapter young men could study with profit.

CALVIN TOMKINS

was born at Orange, N. J., Jan. 31, 1793. His ancestors had emigrated from Connecticut to Newark, N. J., several generations previous, and was part of that ultra-Puritanical colony which made a last attempt to set up a Theocratic form of government in America.

From Newark the colony spread gradually back to the Orange Mountain, and at the base of this hill Enos Tomkins, born 1770, the father of the subject of this sketch, lived and carried on the business of tanning leather and manufacturing shoes. His business was extensive for that time, and his factory gave employment to many people of the neighborhood.

Joseph Tomkins, his grandfather, the son of John Tomkins, lived here also, and was remarkable for liberality in gifts and education. His influence among the farmers was considerable.

Calvin was brought up to work on the farm, and learned his father's trade. He became dissatisfied with this mode of life, and at the age of 16 or 17 years he went to Newark with his pack on his back, where he engaged himself to the managers of the "Bridge Dock" Line of Packets, which plied between Newark and New York. For several years he continued boating on the Passaic and Hudson Rivers.

During the war of 1812 he entered the service, and was stationed for some time at Sandy Hook.

After peace was declared, he returned to boating, and ran for some time between Richmond, Va., and New York city. During one of these voyages he was shipwrecked off Sandy Hook, and suffered temporary illness, brought on by exposure.

About this time (1819) he married Esther Tuers, daughter of Cornelius Tuers, of Barbadoes Neck, as East Newark was then called, and this event put an end to his deep water voyages, although for some time he continued in command of one of the Bridge Dock Packet boats. Domestic ties and business opportunities soon conspired to keep him constantly at Newark.

The introduction of anthracite coal attracted his attention, and he engaged himself in building up a business in the sale of this article.

This led him to set up a kiln for burning lime on the property of the Bridge Dock Co., utilizing the fine coal which at that time was of little value. Both business ventures proved successful.

The coal business increased rapidly, and his efforts to introduce it were rewarded by special concessions from the Pennsylvania Coal Co. The farmers from the surrounding country came in for land lime, and his sales were increased.

He also added to his business the manufacture of plaster and cement, and since it now assumed proportions too large for his own immediate supervision, he associated several of his friends with him and formed " The Newark Lime & Cement Manufacturing Co.," " The Tompkin's Cove Lime Co." and " The Albert Manufacturing Co.," the last-named concern being located in New Brunswick, Canada.

The accomplishment of these enterprises, briefly noticed, was the work of many years, which Mr. Tomkins devoted to them.

After the death of Mrs. Tomkins, he married Mrs. Eliza Parish.

About 1858 he located in Tompkin's Cove, when the beautiful town sprang up about him, mainly through his extraordinary efforts for its promotion.

His father, Enos, was born at Orange in 1770, his grandfather Joseph being a native of the same town. Remarkably, too, his great-grandfather, John Tomkins, was also born here. His mother's maiden name was Sarah Condit; his grandmother's was Desire Freman.

The brothers of Calvin Tomkins were Elias, David, Ambros, Daniel and Enos; sisters were Sarah, Lydia and Elmira. The children of this Patriarch are Walter, Joseph, Cornelius, Sarah, Jane, Phoebe and Laura; his sons-in-law are J. G. Lindsley, H. Lincoln, Jas. Hill and Geo. S. Wood.

His daughters-in-law are Augusta Baldwin, Augusta Macent and Kate Lefferts.

The grandchildren were Laura, Gertrude, Dwight, Calvin, Walter, William, Anna Amelia, Esther, Calvin Hill, Annie Lindsley, Katie Aldie.

Mr. Tomkins is a sturday Republican, a staunch Methodist and an earnest Temperance worker.

He is a man of wide of wide reputation, of extensive possessions, and, besides great liberality to his denomination in gifts and endowments, he enjoys the love and confidence of a large circle of friends, who will arise in the last day to call him blessed.

EBENEZER MC KENZIE,

the grandfather of H. B. McKenzie, was one of the Revolutionary

Fathers, having emigrated from the Highlands of Scotland about the year 1760, landing on Nantucket Island, and from thence came to Stony Point in 1776. He served during the eight years of the War, and was among the cantonment discharged at Newburg, June 10, 1783, his discharge bearing the signature of General George Washington. The widow of the patriot McKenzie, received $1400 pension in 1832.

In 1796, Mr. McKenzie was commissioned captain of a company, as shown in the following commission, the original of which Mr. H. B. McKenzie has in his possession, viz.:

"The People of the State of New York, By the Grace of God, Free and Independent, to Ebenezer McKenzie, Greeting: We, reposing especial trust and confidence as well in your patriotism, conduct and loyalty, as in your valour and readiness to do us good and faithful service, have appointed and constituted, and by these Presents do appoint and constitute you, the said Ebenezer McKenzie, Ensign of a Company in the Regiment of Militia in the County of Orange, whereof Seth Marvin, Esq., is Lieutenant-Colonel Commandant. You are, therefore, to take the said Company into your charge and care as Ensign thereof, and duly to exercise the officers and soldiers of that Company in arms, who are hereby commanded to obey you as their Ensign, and you are also to observe and follow such orders and directions as you shall from time to time receive from our General and Commander-in-Chief of the Militia of our said State, or any other your superior officers, according to the rules and discipline of war; in pursuance of the trust reposed in you, and for so doing this shall be your commission for and during our good pleasure, to be signified by our council of appointment. In testimony whereof, we have caused our Seal for Military Commissions to be hereunto affixed. Witness our trusty and well-beloved John Jay, Esquire, Governor of the State of New York, General and Commander-in-Chief of all the Militia, and Admiral of the Navy of the same, by and with the counsel and consent of our said council of appointment at our said City of New York, the twenty-fourth day of March, in the year of our Lord one thousand seven hundred and ninety-six, and in the twentieth year of our Independence. Passed the Secretary's office the fifth day of April, 1796. Lewis A. Scott, Secretary.

"John Jay, Orange Co., ss.:

"This may certify that on the 25th day of June, 1796, the within-named Ebenezer McKenzie appeared before me and took and subscribed the necessary Oaths prescribed by law, to qualify him to the office within mentioned.

"REUBEN HOPKINS, Clerk of Orange County."

DAVID M. TORREY.

The life of the subject of the following sketch is probably, in some respects, the most remarkable of any in the memory of the reader, so much so that we feel justified and fortunate in having procured the facts for special use in our delineation of self-made men, hoping that the publication of this brief outline will be an incentive to a determined application of the talent and time to worthy pursuits of other young men.

Mr. David M. Torrey, our esteemed friend and successful financier, has had a marvelous career. He was born in Oneida County, N. Y., in 1847. Leaving the district school in 1865, he went to Cazenovia Seminary in Madison County, where he remained one year. In 1867 his uncle, David Manning, a banker of Oswego, procured for him a position in the First National Bank. Here, during three years, he obtained knowledge which should be of help to him in all the after years of his business life. Like many other aspiring young men, he went West in search of a broader field of labor. There he engaged in banking with J. D. Briggs, of Warsaw, Mo. In 1870 he married Miss D. S. Briggs, the banker's daughter. The West was at that time too dull for the business genius and push of the young man, and he turned his face to the Metropolis, with the hope of finding an opening in his line of business. The great panic of 1875 was just about closing. Ten thousand clerks stood ready to accept positions of lowest pay. Mr. Torrey found himself in the great city, almost unknown and without money.

At this time (1876) Mr. Moody was holding the famous hippodrome meetings, and as Mr. Torrey had nothing to engage his time when not seeking for work, he was induced to accompany a friend to the Revival meetings. The Word of God dropped like a precious seed into the mind of the despondent man. And these were the words the preacher used: "Take God at His Word for salvation." Instantly it flashed upon his mind that if God could be trusted for salvation spiritually, why not temporally. He said, "This is what I want. I will trust the Heavenly Father. Every other attempt at procuring help has failed me. I am in despair. I can lose nothing by trying." He entered the inquiry room, and found peace by believing. A great change came over his entire plans. Day after day, by request of Mr. Moody, he employed his time assisting in the meeting. He determined to seek first the Kingdom of God, believing that every other blessing would come.

Assistance came; but it was only loaned; he has since paid it all back. It was his only ambition to please God. He continued daily in the meetings from February until April 15. Three days after the meetings closed the light of business prosperity broke suddenly upon his path. The Word of God was being fulfilled to him. The beginning was feeble, but success crowned every advancing step. He borrowed $85 from his father-in-law. With this roll of greenbacks, satchel in hand, he went from place to place and bought up fractional currency, which the Government had now begun to redeem in new silver coin. A banker by trade, he abode in the same calling wherein he was called. "The business needed men of integrity." The profits were one per cent., so the first day he made eighty-five cents. The second day his receipts doubled. In a short time his business required an office. At first he hired simply a desk in an office, which was in a third story in Wall Street, and afterwards in Ann Street. His business increased, until his satchel had carried tons of trade dollars and foreign silver. In 1885 he opened his present office, corner of Ann and Nassau Streets, where, during the course of the year, millions of money passes through his hands.

Mr. Torrey, with his wife and daughter, Daisy M., now occupies a comfortable home in Brooklyn, and enjoys the confidence of a widely increasing circle of financial and business men. His business is recognized as of great commercial importance, and facilitates the development of the industrial enterprises of the country as scarcely no other business does, the exchange department, the collection of mercantile paper, and the receipt of deposits being indispensible in every city of any considerable size in the country. In the range of business he buys and sells sovereigns, Napoleons, Spanish and Mexican doubloons, Canadian silver, etc.

APPENDIX.

These are specimens of the "clay dogs" referred to on page 81. The engravings are made from photographs taken by Geo. O. Bedford, and are perfect pictures of the original formations in the clay beds.

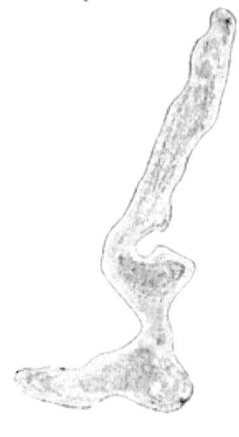
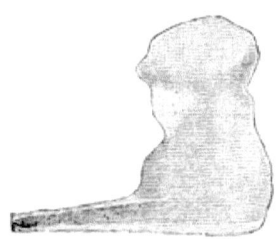

Business Notes.

Household and Wearing Apparel.

W. T. Purdy and Heman M. Purdy, under the firm name of W. T. Purdy & Son, Main Street, Haverstraw, are dealers in furniture of all kinds; also carpets, oil-cloths and window shades. An undertaking department is also connected with their establishment, which is conducted first-class in every detail. W. T. Purdy, with 18 years' experience, will give personal attention in all cases. Prices and satisfaction in both departments guaranteed.

☞ We buy our silk hats of Charles Gates, 70 Barclay and 229 Greenwich Streets, N. Y.

J. S. Coward, maker of wide, easy shoes for everybody. Prices within reach of all. 270 Greenwich St., N. Y.

Music and Art.

It is a sufficient advertisement for the artistic and courteous photographer, Geo. O. Bedford, of Haverstraw, to say that the engravings (of this volume), made by the great Metropolitan "Photo Engraving Company," 67 Park Place, are taken from the plates made by Mr. Bedford. Many of them were taken on severely cold days in December. The snow scenes are beautiful pictures of nature.

The far-famed Bradbury Piano!—Testimonials are published coming from the departments of the Executive Mansion, the Bureau of the Navy, many of the leading hotels, seminaries and churches, giving general praise of the superior instruments made by F. G. Smith. His recently improved uprights are gems of beauty and are unsurpassed for tone. His prices defy competition. Apply for catalogue. Address—F. G. Smith, cor. Raymond and Willoughby Sts., Brooklyn, N. Y.—*Rev. W. R. Kiefer, Author.*

The Alleger Organ is now one of the cheapest and best-toned instruments in the market. It will pay any one about to invest in an organ to call and see one of Mr. Alleger's at the house of John W. Vanwort. For prices, which are in the reach of everyone, call on the publisher of this History, or address H. W. Alleger, Washington, N. J.

This cut represents the New American Roller Organ, which is the greatest contrivance in the music of this age. It plays any tune arranged for it. The rolls of music are in cylinder shape, and have only to be lifted out when another tune is to be inserted. It plays 260 tunes, sentimental and sacred. The customer can select. They are all one price. Special agents wanted in every town. Price $6. Address—World Manuf. Co., 122 Nassau St., N. Y.

Lavalette Wilson, A. M., Civil Engineer and Surveyor, has had over twenty years experience in Rockland County. Surveys, measurements and estimates of all kinds made with accuracy and despatch. Distant points at early hours by trains on the West Shore and N. J. & N. Y. Rail Roads.

Literature.

Harper & Bros. is the most popular, if not the largest publishing house in the city. Its publications are known over the globe. Any work bearing the imprint of Harper & Bros. will sell and be read.

J. LEACH, stationer, printer and blank book manufacturing, 86 Nassau Street, New York. Writing inks, letter, note, foolscap, bill and legal cap; all sizes of cash boxes; standard American and spring back diaries on hand all the year; all kinds of Esterbrook's Gillott's, Perry's Spencerian, Washington medalion steel pens, ball pointed, etc.; Leach's falcon and law pens. One price only. Established 1856.

For cheap, new and desirable books call at the immense book emporium of Phillips & Hunt, 805 Broadway. Just out, "Principles of Church Government," by Perrine; "Christianity in the United States from the First Settlements down," by D. Dorchester; "The Life of Punshon," by McDonald Christopher; and "Other Stories," by Amelia E. Barr; "Gold and Dross," by J. W. Spear; "The Life of John Wesley," by Telford; "Probationer's Hand Book," "Days and Nights on the Sea;" a superb work entitled "The Modern Sunday School," by Dr. Vincent.

MEDICAL.

DR. E. MARQUEZ, of Bogota, U. S. of Colombia, South America, stands deservedly high in the profession and practice of dentistry, and during the time he has been established here in Haverstraw, he has won a leading and prominent rank. Dr. Marquez has commodious rooms, located on Main Street, formerly occupied by Dr. Crawford, there being every convenience which modern science has invented for the speedy and accurate performance of all operations required. Gas is given to those whose constitutions are strong enough to endure it, and as little pain is inflicted as the nature of the case will allow. The doctor attends to all branches of his profession, executing orders for false teeth, in the manufacture of which he excels pre-eminently. He has made and placed in the patient's mouth full and entire sets of teeth, which have all the beauty and usefulness of natural teeth. He is sympathizing in his nature, and shrinks from causing more pain than is absolutely necessary. In every respect his establishment is deserving of the confidence of the public.— *W. R. Kiefer.*

The Linament used with such wonderful results since we have introduced it in this place is now sold by J. B. HASTINGS, at Tomkins' Bros. store. Inquire for Townsend's "V. P. D." Linament. The trial of a bottle is all the notice we need make of it. Its sale is wonderfully increasing.— *Publisher of History.*

☞ An Important Notice! To any one suffering from paralysis, a disease for which the ordinary physician has no remedy, the announcement of Mrs. Dr. E. C. BAIRD's opening the "Cornell Rest" will be hailed as a special providence in behalf of suffering humanity. Spacious apartments will be added to the Birdsall House, at Cornwall Landing, where Mrs. Baird has made a large purchase for her establishment and hospital. Her treatments are oils, food and rest. No parent need fear to leave in the tender care of Mrs. Baird an infant that is a paralytic or constitutionally weak. Its recovery is almost a positive certainty. Address—Mrs. Dr. E. C. Baird, Cornwall Landing, N. Y.

FINANCIAL.

Haverstraw People's Bank, whose charter dates from Feb. 19, 1887, has had a prosperity unparalleled in the history of the country. Its annual statement will be a genuine surprise to all who were so fortunate as to get stock in this new and popular institution. For business purposes address C. F. WASHBURN, President, or H. C. VER VALEN, Cashier, Haverstraw, N. Y.

REAL ESTATE.

Now for sale, at a great bargain, a house on 13th Street, Brooklyn. House cost $4,500; will sell for $3,600. Apply to BURRILL & DRIVER, 5th Ave., Brooklyn, N. Y.

AGENCIES.

W. T. WEIANT, agent for Cleveland Paper Co.'s flour sacks, Delphu's Paper Co.'s XX straw, Peasley's Stone Ridge and grocers straw papers; paper bags, Manila paper, butter dishes, flour sacks, straw paper, tissue paper, toilet paper, tea paper, skewers, twines, printing, stationery, etc. Address—W. T. Weiant, Haverstraw, N. Y.

Refreshments.

Fuller's Broadway Restaurant, Haverstraw, N. Y. Ladies' and gents' oyster and dining rooms. Oysters and clams by 100 or 1,000. Ice cream, wholesale and retail; church fairs, festivities, excursions and the trade supplied at short notice. B. A. Fuller.

Mrs. Minnie Linch keeps confections and ice cream at Conner's Corner.

Mr. Henry Hahn, the Broadway grocer, Haverstraw, will take your order and deliver your goods twice a week and oftener. His wagon makes regular trips through Stony Point. Goods just as cheap as they can be had in the store. Try him to satisfy yourself.

A. Mayers, confectioner, wholesale and retail, complies with New York prices. Churches, picnics, Sunday schools and social gatherings supplied at short notice. Be sure to call before going elsewhere. Broadway, Haverstraw, N. Y.

www.ingramcontent.com/pod-product-compliance
Lightning Source LLC
Chambersburg PA
CBHW020311170426
43202CB00008B/571